Back Lane Wineries
of
SONOMA

BACK LANE
WINERIES
OF
SONOMA

TILAR MAZZEO

THE LITTLE BOOKROOM ✦ NEW YORK

© 2009 The Little Bookroom

Text © 2009 Tilar J. Mazzeo

Photographs: Paul Hawley

Design: Jessica Hische / Louise Fili Ltd

Library of Congress Cataloging-in-Publication Data

Mazzeo, Tilar J.

Back lane wineries of Sonoma County / by Tilar J. Mazzeo.

p. cm.

Includes index.

ISBN 978-1-892145-69-7 (alk. paper)

1. Wine tourism— California— Sonoma County. 2. Wine tasting—

California—Sonoma County. 3. Travel —Guidebooks. I. Title.

TP548.5.T68M39 2008

641.2'20979418 — dc22

2008024238

Published by The Little Bookroom

435 Hudson Street, 3rd Floor • New York NY 10014

editorial@littlebookroom.com • littlebookroom.com

Distributed by Random House

Printed in China

Photo Credits:

p. 83, 84-85: © Sausal Vineyards and Winery.

p. 89, 90-91, 92, 93: © Wattle Creek Winery; Mikala Kennan, photographer.

p. 94, 95, 96, 97, 98: © Garden Creek Ranch Vineyard Winery.

p. 140, 142-143: © Lynmar Estate; Annabelle Breakey, photographer.

p. 146, 147: © Pellegrini Family Vineyards.

p. 186: © VJB Vineyards and Cellars.

TABLE of CONTENTS

INTRODUCTION

THE WINES IN SONOMA COUNTY ARE WORLD-CLASS, AND EACH YEAR OVER 7.5 MILLION TOURISTS VISIT WHAT LOCALS call simply the North Bay—the rural and still magical wine country less than an hour north of San Francisco. As everyone knows, of course, wine tasting is a serious business. Swirl, sniff, taste. There is nothing wrong with classiness and expertise and the love of a fine wine. This is the stuff *la dolce vita* is made of.

The wine country is also, increasingly, big business. Many tasting rooms are slick retail operations run by corporate managers living somewhere a long way from Sonoma, offering wines that you can buy just as readily (and often less expensively) on the shelves of your local grocery store. Often, these are beautiful places, and I am not recommending that you pass them by entirely. A part of the California wine tasting experience is sitting on marbled Italianate terraces overlooking acres of perfectly pruned vineyards, basking in the warm sun and the intense loveliness of it all.

But you don't need a guidebook to see this part of the North Bay wine country. Highway 101 is plastered with billboards, and you would be hard pressed to miss the big-name tasting rooms clustered around the central plazas of quaint towns like Sonoma, Healdsburg, or Glen Ellen (all worth a leisurely visit).

Just as exciting and often far more difficult to spot, however, are the small, back lane wineries of Sonoma, places that the critics, industry professionals, and locals revere but that few visitors ever see. These are wineries run by the same people who grow the grapes and make the wines, and they are geared toward curious travelers, looking to discover what it is about Sonoma County that makes everyone who lives here swear that it is paradise.

This is a guide to those back lane wineries of Sonoma. Places where you can find excellent handcrafted wines made by on-site proprietors, often with only a local or regional distribution and a limited case production. The vast majority of the wineries included in this book make fewer than ten thousand cases of wine a year, and the smallest produce only a hundred or so. The largest make fewer than thirty-five thousand cases, and, in a county where some of the big commercial operations churn out five million cases of wine a year, this is still a small operation. Off the beaten path there are few marble terraces or stucco palaces, but often these wineries are in the midst of striking beauty — overlooking a hundred acres of a wildlife preserve, on the edge of an ancient redwood forest, or simply tucked along a rural side road in the middle of open fields, where the proprietors are happy to watch you settle down for a picnic with a bottle or two of wine.

Best of all, in my mind, these are places where wine tasting gets down to earth. These are places where no one needs to show off how developed his or her palate is and where the winemakers welcome questions, from beginners and experts alike. Often, you will also find that these are the wineries where sustainable and organic viticulture is being pioneered. Above all, these are wines that are likely to be a new experience, with names that you won't find in big retail outlets back home. Amid the back lane wineries of Sonoma, you can still make secret discoveries.

HOW ᴛᴏ USE ᴛʜɪꜱ BOOK

THE SONOMA COUNTY WINE REGION IS MADE UP OF MORE
THAN A DOZEN APPELLATIONS AND SUB-APPELLATIONS,
some of them quite small, each with a particular microclimate
and with particular grape varietals that thrive in the region.
Most of the wineries in the area can be reached by traveling
along one of two local highways, Highway 101, which runs north-south,
or Sonoma Highway (also known simply as Highway 12), which intersects
with Highway 101 near Santa Rosa and runs roughly east-west.

Sonoma County covers a relatively large area, and, because it can
easily take more than an hour of steady driving to get across the region,
the best way to plan a day of wine tasting is to focus on just one or
two appellations, taking time for a leisurely gourmet lunch and some
sightseeing along the way. This guide is arranged by region, and at
the end of each section are suggestions for nearby restaurants or local
attractions that you can work into an itinerary spontaneously.

This book divides the county into five primary areas, which, working
south along Highway 101 include:

- **DRY CREEK VALLEY** (west of Highway 101 at Healdsburg), focusing
  on zinfandel, cabernet, sauvignon blanc; includes the Dry Creek
  Valley and Rockpile American Viticultural Area (A.V.A.)

- **ALEXANDER VALLEY** (northeast of Highway 101 at Healdsburg),
  focusing on cabernet, chardonnay; includes the Alexander Valley and
  Knight's Valley A.V.A.

- **HEALDSBURG** (Highway 101), a charming little boutique town, where many small producers have tasting rooms.

- **RUSSIAN RIVER VALLEY** (west of Highway 101 at Windsor), focusing on chardonnay, pinot noir; includes the Russian River Valley, Sonoma Coast, Green Valley, and Chalk Hill A.V.A.

- **SONOMA**, which encompasses the historic town of Sonoma and the surrounding appellations (east of Highway 101 at Santa Rosa, along Sonoma Highway [12], and south of the town of Sonoma along Highway 121), focusing on cabernet, merlot, zinfandel, pinot noir, chardonnay, as well as sparkling wines in the traditional "Champagne" style; includes the Sonoma Valley, Sonoma Mountain, Bennett Valley, and Los Carneros A.V.A.

All the wineries listed in this book are open to visitors, and wine-tasting hours throughout the county are generally from 10 AM − 4:30 PM daily, although some wineries have longer or shorter hours, and it is always a good idea to call ahead to confirm opening times, especially early in the week (Monday and Tuesday particularly). Groups larger than six people should always call ahead to be sure the winemakers can accommodate you.

Many of the best small wineries are open by appointment only, and you should not feel in the least bit shy about making the call. It just means that the winemaker wants to be sure he or she knows to staff the tasting room that afternoon, and it is usually a sign that the person behind the bar will be the same person who goes out pruning the vines other days of the week. Often these winemaker tours are exceptional educational experiences and a rare opportunity to get an inside perspective on the craft of winemaking. Generally, it's a good idea to call a week in advance of your trip to set up appointments (and at a few places there are long waiting lists, which are noted in the particular entries). But should you find yourself in the wine country unexpectedly, there's absolutely no harm in making a spur-of-the-moment call. Often, the winemakers are able to welcome even last-minute visitors.

When you are planning your trip, keep in mind that weekends are the busiest time for wine tasting, especially at the commercial wineries and in summer, where you will often have to jostle for a place at the tasting bar. A busy Saturday is the perfect time to head off the beaten path and visit some of the back lane wineries. Locals prefer to go wine tasting on Thursdays and Friday mornings, when most places are open and gearing up for the weekend. If you are planning to visit in September, plan with particular care: The harvest — known in Sonoma County simply as "the crush" — takes place around then, and the tasting room hours can be limited, but there are often opportunities to participate in other special events and harvest suppers during what can be one of the most festive times of the winemaking year.

And what will all this cost? Many tasting rooms (and nearly all the commercial ones) charge modest tasting fees, ranging from five to ten dollars for a "flight" of wines — usually a small taste of about a half-dozen different wines. It generally costs a bit more to taste "reserve" wines ($20 and up is common), and the best of those experiences are sit-down private appointments with a winemaker that can last an hour or more. If you want to visit several wineries, no one will mind in the least if you ask to share a flight with your tasting companions, and in most cases the cost of your tasting fees will be waived if you buy even a single bottle of wine.

In some places, especially in the smaller back road wineries, there will be no charge for tasting and no charge even for the winemaker tours, and there is never any obligation to buy wine when out tasting. But winemaking is an expensive business and for many of these small proprietors this is a labor of love. Buying someone's wine after you've enjoyed it is the best compliment, and my own rule of thumb for wine tasting etiquette is that, if there is no charge for the tasting, the polite thing to do is buy a bottle or two. When there is a charge for the tasting, I only buy the wines I know I will enjoy. But because tasting fees are so often waived with a purchase, it never makes any sense to me not to buy a bottle at each winery.

If you don't have room to take it home, many of the best local restaurants here in wine country charge only a modest corkage fee for opening your own special bottle tableside. In Sonoma County, gourmet food is one of the great community passions. Almost every day of the week in the summer there are open-air farmers markets in the local town squares, where families gather to listen to jazz on cool evenings and dine *al fresco* out of their canvas shopping bags. The grocery stores offer a dizzying array of homemade cheese and artisan breads, and the local park rangers offer classes in mushroom hunting each autumn. But when it comes to food, the North Bay wine country is most famous for its restaurants—and rightly so. The restaurant recommendations in this guide highlight places where you are welcome to enjoy your most recent discovery—places that also have excellent local wine lists, where perhaps new discoveries await. In a corner of the world blessed with an abundance of riches, these are also the kind of restaurants where you can while away a long afternoon when the pressures of wine tasting become overwhelming or where you can settle in for a lovely dinner worth celebrating.

WINE TASTING ESSENTIALS

EVEN SOPHISTICATED WINE AFICIONADOS SOMETIMES FIND THEMSELVES WONDERING WHAT THE "RIGHT" WAY TO TASTE wine is, and as you anticipate sitting down face-to-face with a winemaker it's easy to start worrying about whether you'll pass the test. There's no need: In the wine country, the friendliest welcome of all is reserved for passionate amateurs. And you're not the only one who gets the giggles when that gentleman at the far end of the tasting bar starts throwing around wildly improbable adjectives. The winemakers do too.

However, if you want to refresh yourself on the basics before throwing yourself into your wine tasting adventures, it's easily done. For starters, hold the wine glass by the stem. Cupping it in your hands and leaving greasy fingerprints not only looks decidedly unglamorous, but this will also warm the wine, changing its aromas. The experts will tell you that "tasting" wine is largely about aroma. We can only experience six different tastes, and nature's way around the limited range of our taste buds is to marry those perceptions to the thousand or more different smells that we can detect, creating seemingly endless delights for the gourmet. This is the whole point of swirling and sniffing your wine.

When you are handed a glass — and your tasting typically will progress from the lightest wine to the most intense wine in the flight — begin by gently tilting it to look at the clarity and colors, if you like. Unless you're an expert, the conclusion you'll probably reach is that it looks delicious, but a trained eye will be looking to assess alcohol content, barrel aging, and structural components. Then, give the glass a swirl. Many of us accomplish this most gracefully by keeping the glass on the table and making a few quick circles, but if you're the daring sort there's always the riskier mid-air execution to perfect as the afternoon wears on. The point is that the movement begins to open the bouquet of the wine. You are supposed to start with a gentle sniff with your nose above the glass, then move on to a deeper sniff with your nose right down there in the stemware. As a wine drinker and not a contest judge, what you're looking for is a sensory experience that will help you pick out the different aromas that are going to shape how this wine is going to taste for you.

The next step — finally — is to take a sip of wine. But remember that the taste buds are in your mouth and not down your gullet. So roll the wine around in your mouth for a few moments, making sure it reaches the different parts of your tongue, where the distinct tastes and textures are experienced. Before you swallow, you can also try pulling a little air over your teeth and breathing in through your nose to aspirate the wine and intensify the experience of the aroma.

There is also a technique where you can attempt to slurp the wine silently and draw the vapors into your sinuses, usually effected by placing your tongue on the outside of the glass as you drink and inhaling simultaneously. If you do it right, the result is what the experts call retro-olfaction — a concentrated explosion of aroma that takes the information your brain needs to process smell more directly to your neurological receptors, but if you do it wrong, you'll end up sputtering wine rather dramatically. It might be wise to practice at home first, or if you find yourself wine tasting without an audience, ask one of the winemakers you'll meet out in the far corners of Sonoma County to show you how it's done.

You may also see some fellow tasters spit the wine out without swallowing in the course of your tasting adventures. That's perfectly acceptable, and it's the reason tasting rooms all have those dump buckets on the counter. All those little sips of wine add up quickly, after all.

SHIPPING WINES HOME

~~~

FOR MANY VISITORS TO THE WINE COUNTRY OF SONOMA COUNTY, THE TROUBLE IS FINDING WAYS TO GET ALL THESE wonderful wines home. And when you have been touring the back lane wineries, discovering small-production, handcrafted wines that won't be available at home, the question takes on a particular urgency. Most of the wineries in this book distribute their wines only through their tasting-room sales, and this is part of what makes discovering them so satisfying.

Depending on where you live, there are several excellent options for getting your purchases back to your home cellar. Many wineries will ship your purchases home to you directly, provided your state allows this. The costs are generally prohibitive for a single bottle of wine, but for several it is quite reasonable. For purchases of a case or more, ask whether there is flexibility in their wine club program. The discounts are significant, and generally your only commitment is agreeing to purchase a case of wine over the course of the year. Often, the wineries want to ship the wines to you quarterly, but, when we wanted to get a few cases to our summer place in New England, I never had any trouble persuading the local winemakers to send me the entire annual allotment at once, at a significant savings in the shipping.

Another option is to send it as checked luggage. We have done it for years and only very rarely has a bottle broken *en route*. A sturdy cardboard box, marked fragile, can get an entire case of wine across the country with minimal hassle, provided you understand the airline policies and your state sales-tax regulations. Most wineries will happily give you a regular packing box, and some of the wineries have started selling extra-sturdy boxes specifically designed for sending wines this way. You can also purchase a wine lover's suitcase from catalogue suppliers before your trip and rest easy knowing that your only worry is finding favorite wines to fill it up.

And for those extra special, high-end purchases destined for the cellars of the serious collector, there are always third-party shippers who specialize in sending wines anywhere you need them to go. On page 238, I list my favorite ones, or you can ask at any premium winery for the staff recommendations.

Even if you take nothing home with you as a souvenir for your cellar, the back lane wineries of Sonoma are an experience few visitors ever forget. Off the beaten path and along the back roads, amid oak trees and mustard blooms, the experience of wine tasting is immediate and personal. May your journey and discoveries be as individual as your palate, and welcome to the heart of Sonoma County.

CHAPTER ONE

DRY CREEK VALLEY

This little sliver of a valley in northern Sonoma County is home to some of California's finest zinfandels, which thrive in the dry, hot summers in this part of the wine country. The appellation is also known for its excellent cabernet sauvignon, merlot, and — increasingly — its less familiar Italian and southern French varietals.

When tasting in the appellation, it is easy to confuse Dry Creek Road with West Dry Creek Road. The two run roughly parallel to each other in a north-south direction through the valley, and both roads are home to some of the region's best back lane discoveries. You could do a full day of tasting on either route. But, for dedicated wine enthusiasts, my favorite circuit begins by taking the Dry Creek exit from Highway 101, tasting your way north along Dry Creek Road as far as Yoakim Bridge Road, which heads west and intersects with West Dry Creek Road. If you then taste your way south on West Dry Creek Road, you can either call it quits and head back to Highway 101 via Lambert Bridge Road or continue south until West Side Road. You can pick up free road maps at almost any tasting room or hotel in the wine country.

WILSON WINERY

1960 Dry Creek Road ✦ Healdsburg
Exit Dry Creek Road west *from* Highway 101.
Tasting daily 11AM *to* 5PM
Tel: 707.433.4355 ✦ www.wilsonwinery.com

TRAVELING ALONG DRY CREEK ROAD, ONE OF THE FIRST WINERIES YOU'LL COME TO IS A HUNDRED-YEAR-OLD TIN barn with a sign that invites you to come visit Wilson Winery. When you're eager to see what the valley has to offer, it's easy to keep driving. After all, you're thinking, let's see what's out there; we can always come back.

But who knows where the day is going to take you, and it would be a shame to miss out tasting the small-lot wines crafted by Diane and Ken Wilson. The couple has brought home from the harvest fairs and the international competitions one award after another. In 2005 alone, Diane's signature zinfandels won gold medals from the National Women's Wine Competition, the West Coast Wine Competition, the Orange County Fair Wine Competition, the Los Angeles International Wine Competition, the Sonoma County Harvest Fair, and the *San Francisco Chronicle* Wine Competition. If, for some crazy reason, zinfandel just isn't your thing, the Wilson family also crafts excellent, award-winning cabernet sauvignon, cabernet franc, petite sirah, and syrah wines ($30 to $50 range), grown on over two hundred acres of estate vineyards that start out the back door. The long views over the valley from the tasting room alone are worth the visit.

NALLE WINERY

2383 Dry Creek Road ✦ Healdsburg
Exit Dry Creek Road west *from* Highway 101.
Winery is south *of the* Lytton Springs Road intersection.
Tasting Saturday 12PM *to* 5PM *or* by appointment
Tel: 707.433.1040 ✦ www.nallewinery.com

THE SELF-PROCLAIMED MOTTO OF THE NALLE FAMILY IS "VINUM SAPIENTIAM TIBI DAT." FOR ANYONE WHOSE Latin is a bit on the rusty side that roughly translates to "wine makes you smart." And it's those handy opposable thumbs — so perfect for holding wine glasses — that separate us from the primordial pollywogs. It's all just part of nature's "zintelligent design." Or that's what one of the witty t-shirts displayed in the winery's tasting room announces.

This laidback and fun-loving approach — combined with a single-minded passion for making great wines — is what the Nalle family winery, run by Lee and Doug Nalle and their son Andrew, is all about. There's nothing stuffy or pretentious here about wine or winemaking. They have been quietly making acclaimed small-lot wines since the early 1980s, and their tast-

ing room is also a working winery and barrel room. In fact, it is one of Sonoma County's few above-ground *caves* — the building is covered with sod and planted with the fragrant rosemary that grows so easily in the North Bay's Mediterranean climate. The purpose of this unique structure, however, is all about winemaking: the soil creates an ideal climate for aging wines, naturally regulating both the temperature and the humidity in a fashion that is at once traditional and ecologically sustainable.

Despite the ironic irreverence of the wine marketing at Nalle, the wines ($35–45 range) are nothing but serious. Their zinfandel, a Dry Creek Valley classic, is made from the field blend of eighty-year-old vines growing right out in front of the tasting room. With grapes from the Hopkins Ranch vineyard in the Russian River Valley, they also produce a chardonnay and an excellent Burgundy-style pinot noir.

MAURITSON FAMILY WINERY

2859 Dry Creek Road ✦ Healdsburg
Exit Dry Creek Road west *from* Highway 101.
Winery is *at the* Lytton Springs Road intersection.
Tasting daily 10AM *to* 5PM;
winemaker *and* vineyard tours by appointment
Tel: 707.431.0804 ✦ www.mauritsonwines.com

YOU MIGHT FIND YOURSELF THINKING THAT CLAY MAURITSON—THE THIRTY-SOMETHING FORCE BEHIND THE MAURITSON Family Winery — is part of a new generation of winemakers in Sonoma County. Certainly there is nothing old-fashioned or stuffy about the elegant and gleaming tasting rooms where he'll welcome you to sample some wines.

However, the Mauritson family are anything but newcomers in this valley, and Clay is the sixth generation to raise grapes on the estate properties. In fact, just a bit further north, in the newly designated (and aptly named) Rockpile appellation, his pioneering Swedish ancestors planted the first vines in the area back in the 1880s. Much of that sprawling ranch land today lies at the bottom of Lake Sonoma, but Clay — along with his wife Carrie and his dad Thomas — continue to make distinctive zinfandel, syrah, and petite sirah wines (most in the $30 to $45 range) from fruit grown in the high-elevation vineyards that survived. If you've never tried a wine from the Rockpile appellation, you're in for a treat. It's a sparse and rugged landscape, where the vines suffer and the fruit is beautifully intense.

There are also estate wines made from fruit grown on family properties

in the Dry Creek and Alexander Valley appellations, including a small-lot chardonnay and a sauvignon blanc that *Wine Enthusiast* called "one of the purest expressions of unoaked, non-malolactic Sauvignon Blanc in California" (August 2006). At under $20, it's also a good bargain.

AMISTA VINEYARDS

3320 Dry Creek Road ✦ Healdsburg

Exit Dry Creek Road west *from* Highway 101.

Winery is north *of the* Lytton Springs Road intersection.

Tasting Thursday *to* Monday 11AM *to* 4:30PM

Tel. 707.431.9200 ✦ www.amistavineyards.com

MICHAEL AND VICKY FARROW FIRST STARTED DREAMING OF A LIFE IN THE DRY CREEK WINE COUNTRY BACK WHEN they were young and first dating. On one romantic trip to the area, they fell in love with Sonoma County, but life had other career plans for the couple. But even then they had planted the backyard of their suburban home in the Santa Clara Valley with 150 cabernet vines, and Mike started making garage wines for their family and friends.

And Mike and Vicky will tell you that friends have always been at the heart of this enterprise. The name Amista — which roughly translates in Spanish as "making friends" — is a nod to all the people along the way who encouraged them to pursue this shared passion. In 1999, they finally bought twenty-eight acres of ranch land on the eastern banks of the Dry Creek Valley, and in 2003 — at the age when most folks are beginning to dream of retirement — they released their first commercial vintage. Today, their rustic barn-style tasting room lies down the end of a long gravel lane set up against the foothills, and, with the help of their consulting winemaker, Chris Wills, the couple produces around fifteen hundred cases a year of Dry Creek classics: a sauvignon blanc, a chardonnay, a syrah, a cabernet sauvignon, and a zinfandel, all in the $20 to $40 range.

RUED WINES

3850 Dry Creek Road ✦ Healdsburg
Exit Dry Creek Road west *from* Highway 101.
Winery is north *of the* Lambert Bridge Road intersection.
Tasting daily 11AM *to* 4:30PM
Tel: 707.433.3261 ✦ www.ruedvineyards.com

THE RUED WINES TASTING ROOM IS ONE OF THE NEW ADDITIONS TO THE DOZEN OR MORE WINERIES THAT HAVE opened up along Dry Creek Road, but Richard Rued, his wife Dee, and their children have long ties to the Sonoma Valley. Richard—who pours wine in a cowboy hat and could give Clint Eastwood a run for his money in the rugged charm department—got his start as a grower and a rancher back in the fifties, when he grew grapes and prunes as part of a high school agricultural project. For a long while the family turned their attention to raising cherries, beef, and hay just to the east in the Alexander Valley, on the property that great-granddad Rued was running as a vineyard from the 1880s until Prohibition shut him down.

Today, the family grows grapes on land in the Dry Creek, Alexander, and Russian River Valleys, selling most of it on to other local winemakers but since 2000 producing 4,000 cases of 100% estate-grown sauvignon blanc, chardonnay, pinot noir, and zinfandel wines in the $15 to $35 range. Their limited-production sauvignon blanc tastes like spring itself and recently took a gold at the *San Francisco Chronicle* International Wine Judging Competition.

UNTI VINEYARDS

4202 Dry Creek Road ✦ Healdsburg
Exit Dry Creek Road west *from* Highway 101.
Winery is north *of the* Lambert Bridge Road intersection.
Tasting daily 10AM *to* 4PM, by appointment
Tel: 707.433.5590 ✦ www.untivineyards.com

IF YOU START ASKING THE LOCALS FOR RECOMMENDATIONS ABOUT WHOSE WINE YOU CAN'T MISS IN THE DRY CREEK VALLEY, one name that you'll keep hearing is Unti Vineyards. It's a testament to the friendly spirit of Sonoma winemakers and to the warm welcome awaiting visitors down at the end of this dusty back lane.

The family — George, Linda, and Mick — have been producing wines commercially since 1997, and the emphasis on northern Italian and southern French wines is a nod in two directions: to the Unti family's roots in Tuscany and to Mick's passion for the wines of Provence and the Côtes du Rhône. Besides, as Mick will tell you with a warm smile, the climate of the Dry Creek Valley A.V.A. is ideally suited to traditional Mediterranean varieties. Grapes like grenache and mourvèdre or barbera and vermentino will someday become California classics, he predicts. Unti Vineyards is leading the way in this delicious revolution.

Here, the emphasis isn't on a house style but on the expression of *terroir*, though always with an international twist. With winemaker Sébastien Pochan, Mick makes somewhere on the order of seven thousand cases of estate reds, all grown in vineyards that have been farmed using sustainable and biodynamic techniques. Best of all, these are wines priced for the world market, and no one is asking you

to pay inflated boutique prices. Their dry rosé ($18)—a grenache and mourvèdre blend—was inspired by a trip to Nice, where this traditional Provençal wine is served at sidewalk bistros with pizza, and if I could have just one summer afternoon wine this would be it. Unti Vineyards is perhaps best known for its red grenache blend, which has the kind of complexity more commonly associated with a Châteauneuf du Pape or Gigondas—and they are one of the few estates in the New World to work intensively with the varietal. However, there is also a hearty barbera that could stand up to any steak on the grill, along with zinfandel, syrah, and their signature "Segromino"—a sangiovese blend. Most wines are in the $20 to $30 range, and if you want a vineyard tour just ask when you call for an appointment.

PAPAPIETRO PERRY WINERY

4791 Dry Creek Road ✦ Healdsburg
Exit Dry Creek Road west *from* Highway 101.
Winery is north *of the* Lambert Bridge Road intersection.
Tasting daily 11AM *to* 4:30PM
Tel: 707.433.0422 ✦ www.papapietro-perry.com

CLUSTERED TOGETHER UP A STEEP DRIVEWAY ON THE NORTH SIDE OF DRY CREEK ROAD ARE THE TASTING ROOMS and production facilities of nearly a dozen small family wineries, and one of the standouts is the Papapietro Perry Winery, home to some of the most highly acclaimed pinot noir wines you'll find anywhere.

Friends and former newspapermen Ben Papapietro and Bruce Perry first got the idea of making their own wines after they spent a weekend working the crush, and they spent much of the next two decades making wines, in the early days out in the garage using an old hand press. Although they only produced their first commercial vintage in 1998, they already have a world-class reputation, with accolades that include the 2007 *Wine Spectator*'s Critics Choice Award. The focus here is on pinot noir and zinfandel wines in the $35 to $70 range, made from fruit sourced from the best small vineyards in the county.

PETERSON WINERY

4791 Dry Creek Road ✦ Healdsburg
Exit Dry Creek Road west *from* Highway 101.
Winery is north *of the* Lambert Bridge Road intersection.
Tasting daily 11 AM *to* 4:30 PM
Tel: 707.431.7568 ✦ www.petersonwinery.com

RUN BY THE FATHER-AND-SON TEAM OF FRED AND JAMIE PETERSON, THE PETERSON WINERY IS A FRIENDLY, FAMILY affair. Their story started out in the vineyards, where Fred began by supplying grapes to local estates. These days, he says that he still likes to think of himself as a winegrower — someone growing fruit that will make a great wine. And at Peterson, where the philosophy is one of "zero manipulation," the character of the fruit and the land is pretty much everything.

These days, son Jamie is the winemaker, and, if you want to get some hands-on experience as part of your tasting adventure, Peterson Winery offers some of the most intriguing special events in the county. Jamie occasionally offers a wine-blending seminar (around $50, inquiries to friends@petersonwinery.com) where you can learn about how wine is structured and then blend and bottle your own special vintage for enjoyment back home.

But you might want to try some of the wines Jamie has blended first. The *San Francisco Chronicle* recently selected his sangiovese as one of the year's top 100 wines, and other offerings range from cabernet franc and carignane wines to a white muscat dessert wine. There are also familiar favorites like cabernet sauvignon, sauvignon blanc, and a rich array of zinfandels, all in the $10 to $55 range, with most around $25. In fact, zinfandel accounts for nearly half of Peterson Winery's annual production of around five thousand cases. It's the signature wine of the A.V.A., or as Fred puts it: "If you have a winery in the Dry Creek Valley and don't make at least one zinfandel you're stupid, and if it's not really good you should consider a career change! "

TALTY WINERY

7129 Dry Creek Road ✦ Healdsburg
Exit Dry Creek Road west *from* Highway 101.
Winery is just south *of the* Canyon Road intersection.
Tasting *and* vineyard tours by appointment
Tel: 707.433.8438 ✦ www.taltyvineyards.com

BUMPING DOWN THE DIRT ROAD THAT LEADS TO THE TALTY FAMILY TASTING ROOM, YOU DRIVE RIGHT THROUGH THE vineyards, and what you are looking at, Mike Talty will tell you, is the daily love and labor of a man who thinks of himself first and foremost as growing wine not grapes.

Mike and his wife Katie are dedicated to perfecting just one varietal: zinfandel. The family's winery produces less than thirteen hundred cases a year and only two single vineyard designate wines—one an estate zinfandel grown on the seven acres of property out front and the other a Napa County zinfandel made from grapes raised on a two-and-a-half acre parcel they manage over on the other side of Sonoma Mountain.

The fruit here in the Dry Creek Valley comes from forty-five-year-old, head-pruned vines and was once part of one of the large ranches that used to cover the valley floor, although the Talty family only bought the parcel in the late 1990s and released their first vintage in 2001. Almost immediately they made their mark in the wine world when the estate zinfandel was hailed by the *Wall Street Journal* as an undiscovered gem a few years back, and readers were advised, "Remember the name of this Sonoma winery; you'll be hearing it."

But despite all this attention, they still keep things down-to-earth at

Talty Vineyards. It's the kind of place where the tasting bar is a piece of wood propped up on two old oak barrels and where the focus is on just one thing: great handmade wines in the $40 range.

DAVID COFFARO VINEYARD AND WINERY

7485 Dry Creek Road ✦ Geyserville
Exit Dry Creek Road west *from* Highway 101.
Winery is north *of the* Yoakim Bridge Road intersection.
Tasting daily 11AM *to* 4PM; vineyard tours Fridays at 11AM *and* 1PM
Tel: 707.433.9715 ✦ www.coffaro.com

FOR DAVID COFFARO, IT ALL BEGAN WITH BORDEAUX. WORKING IN FINANCE DOWN IN SAN FRANCISCO IN THE 1960s and 1970s, he soon found himself buying wine futures and building a collection. He still remembers with a smile the wine glut of 1970, when prices crashed. He filled his cellars and drank luxuriously for the better part of the next decade. By the early 1980s, David and his wife Pat left the city and purchased twenty-five acres of vineyards on the northern end of the Dry Creek Valley, taking their chances on building a winery in this still undiscovered corner of Sonoma County.

And at David Coffaro wines, it's still all about taking your chances. They produce around five thousand cases of wine a year, and while you can buy from the bottled wines they have on hand when you visit the tasting room, a good part of their annual vintage is sold through what they call their "Crazy Back to the Futures" program—a chance for enthusiastic aficionados and collectors alike to purchase wines early in the season at what generally amounts to a 40% discount or more. It's your chance to pick up a 100% estate-grown cabernet sauvignon that normally retails for $28 for as little as $15.

Because it's all about taking your best guess at what the future is going to bring, the lowest prices are available early in the season (usually April), and a visit to the tasting room generally means bellying up to the barrel. To take some of the guesswork out of it all, the folks at David Coffaro will help you understand exactly what is happening in the barrel and how a wine evolves, and you can always track the progress of a vintage online at David's winemaker's diary (www.coffaro.com/diary). It's a fresh take on daily life in the wine business, and a great way to keep tabs on what to expect from next year's bottles-to-be.

Unlike some other winemakers with futures programs, David and Pat are flexible about when you pick up your wines, or they are happy to ship them if you live outside Sonoma County. And best of all, because David takes some calculated risks in his winemaking as well, you're likely to find some unique and delicious new blends. Zinfandel and cabernet sauvignon are the backbone of the vineyards, but here's also your chance to try — and maybe take an early gamble on — varietals that run the gamut from barbera, petite sirah, and carignane to peloursin, mourvèdre, grenache, petit verdot, tannat, aglianico, or lagrein. For all you dedicated wine lovers, it might just be more fun than a weekend in Las Vegas.

SBRAGIA FAMILY VINEYARDS

9990 Dry Creek Road ✦ Geyserville
Exit Dry Creek Road west *from* Highway 101.
Winery is north *of the* Yoakim Bridge Road intersection.
Tasting daily 11 AM *to* 5 PM
Tel. 707.473.2992 ✦ www.sbragia.com

I N THE CALIFORNIA WINE INDUSTRY, ED SBRAGIA, WHO SPENT HIS CAREER OVER IN NAPA AS THE HEAD WINEMAKER AT Beringer, is something of a legend. Two of the wines he crafted — the 1986 cabernet sauvignon and the 1994 chardonnay — were *Wine Spectator* wines of the year, and for over thirty years lucky collectors around the world have made room for his handiwork in their cellars.

However, making wine and honoring the family's roots in the Dry Creek Valley was also Ed's retirement dream. His grandfather came to California from the graceful little Italian city of Lucca in the first decades of the twentieth century and worked in the wineries. Father Gino eventually saved enough to buy some vineyards, and Ed grew up on the family ranch here in the valley. Even with a job over in Napa, this is where he raised his own kids. Where else would anyone found the Sbragia Family Vineyards?

For the past few years, Ed and his son Adam have been making wines under the new family label — a Dry Creek chardonnay, zinfandel, sauvignon blanc, merlot, and cabernet sauvignon, plus a few chardonnay and cabernet wines made from some special grapes grown over in Napa. As you might expect, the response has been gleeful. The Gamble Ranch chardonnay ranked number 15 on the *Wine Spectator*'s Top 100 Wines list in 2007, and, for those who like to crunch the numbers, these wines are consistently ranked at 90 points or higher. The total production is just under six thousand cases a year, and someday they might go as high as ten thousand. But the idea is always to keep this a labor of love. The wines range from $20 to $75, with most around $30.

The views from the hillside tasting room are spectacular. The Dry Creek Valley floor rolls out for miles on your left, and to the right is the monumental face of the Warm Springs Dam, which holds back the waters of Lake Sonoma.

BELLA VINEYARDS AND WINE CAVES

9711 West Dry Creek Road ✦ Healdsburg
West Dry Creek Road, north *of the* Yoakim Bridge Road intersection
Tasting daily 11AM *to* 4:30PM
Tel: 866.572.3552 ✦ www.bellawinery.com

AT THE VERY NORTHERN END OF THE WEST DRY CREEK ROAD IS THE LITTLE TASTING ROOM AT BELLA VINEYARDS, RUN by Scott and Lynn Adams as part of a larger family wine country venture. The tasting experience — which takes place by candlelight in their echoing underground caves — is one of the most charming and atmospheric you'll find anywhere, and their late harvest zinfandel (around $25) is an excellent wine. In 2007, it took the double gold and medal of class in the *San Francisco Chronicle* Wine Competition.

With a focus on small-lot, handcrafted wines, the emphasis here is exclusively on reds, with other offerings including two zinfandels (one Dry Creek and the other

Alexander Valley) and a cabernet and zinfandel blend (in the $25 to
$40 range) from the Alexander Valley. A tasting flight includes all
four of their wines, and even though it's one of the few places that
won't refund your $5 tasting fee even if you buy a case of wine, it's a
beautiful and hopelessly romantic little spot with some wines that are
definitely worth trying.

PRESTON OF DRY CREEK WINERY AND VINEYARDS

9282 West Dry Creek Road ✦ Healdsburg

West Dry Creek Road, north *of the* Yoakim Bridge Road intersection

Tasting daily 11AM *to* 4:30PM

Tel. 707.433.3372 ✦ www.prestonvineyards.com

WHEN SONOMA COUNTY LOCALS HAVE OUT-OF-TOWN VISITORS TO ENTERTAIN, THERE IS ONE DRY CREEK winery that everyone puts on the itinerary for the perfect wine-country weekend: the rustic extravaganza that is the Preston family winery. Located on the north end of the valley, down a long gravel road that runs along the creek and through ranch land, there is nothing pretentious about the life that Lou and Sue Preston have built here on property they first bought back in the early 1970s. Yet you can't help but think that they've got it all here.

They make wine, of course. In fact, they make excellent wine, with an emphasis on Rhône varietals. Here you can find wines you might not immediately associate with California: grenache blanc, marsanne,

rousanne, viognier, carignane, mourvèdre, even a signature blend with some cinsault. Since all are reasonably priced in the $20 to $30 range, it's a great chance to take your palate on a little trip to the south of France, Dry Creek style, and the $5 tasting fee is refunded with the purchase of a bottle. Although these bottled wines are what you'll need if you want to take it home with you, it's their Guadagni jug wine—named in memory of a beloved neighbor—that makes them a Sonoma County tradition. Available only on Sundays in the tasting room, you can pick up a three-liter jug for less than $35 and drink your way happily through the week on a nice zinfandel, mourvèdre, and carignane blend that will make you wonder why you can't buy table wine like this everywhere in America.

However, as everyone will tell you, wine is just part of the Preston experience. Lou makes what is generally acknowledged to be the best bread in the county, and you can buy warm loaves on the weekends. In the summer, they run their own little farmers market outside the front door of the winery, with sun-ripened heirloom produce grown right here on their organic farm. There are estate-cured olives and olive oils ($32), bocce ball courts where you can engage in a little spirited competition, friendly farm cats looking for ankles to rub, and plenty of space for the impromptu picnic you are almost certain to end up enjoying here in this little corner of paradise.

ZICHICHI FAMILY VINEYARDS

8626 West Dry Creek Road ✦ Healdsburg
West Dry Creek Road, _at the_ Yoakim Bridge Road intersection
Tasting daily 10:30AM _to_ 4:30PM
Tel 707.433.4410 ✦ www.zichichifamilyvineyard.com

STEVE ZICHICHI (PRONOUNCED ZOO-KIKI), A NEW ORLEANS PHYSICIAN, HAD BEEN DREAMING OF A MOVE TO THE WINE country for the better part of a decade when Hurricane Katrina came along. He and his wife Kristin were already avid wine collectors and had purchased twenty-two acres of land here in the Dry Creek Valley, a place they first discovered out wine tasting. After Katrina, they finally took the plunge, crafting their first vintage in 2004 and relocating to California with their four kids in 2006.

Tasting their wines, you find yourself wondering how they have managed to make such a great wine right off the starting block. I asked Steve that question myself when I first discovered their zinfandel during one of the big barrel tasting weekends that have local winemakers throwing open their cellar doors in the spring. This is wine that tastes the way the Dry Creek Valley smells: of warm earth and fresh air. This simple and intense expression of _terroir_ is exactly the idea at Zichichi. The vineyards just beyond the tasting room were planted in the 1920s, and the secret to these wines is a simple one: great land, with great vines, and, Steve will tell you with a laugh, owners who have the good sense not to meddle with what nature has created.

The total production is around four thousand cases a year, with a focus on small-lot red wines, including two estate-grown zinfandels, a cabernet sauvignon, and a petite sirah ($25 to $50 range). From the rustic tasting room, you've got long views over the Dry Creek Valley, and visitors are welcome to bring a picnic.

GÖPFRICH ESTATE VINEYARD AND WINERY

7462 West Dry Creek Road ✦ Healdsburg
West Dry Creek Road, south *of the* Yoakim Bridge Road intersection
Tasting daily by appointment
Tel. 707.433.1645 ✦ www.gopfrich.com

INE TASTING WITH RAY GOEPFRICH——THE MAN BEHIND THE GÖPFRICH ESTATE VINEYARDS——IS A CONVIVIAL affair, where visitors settle in around a big wooden table and get a personal introduction to the 100% estate red wines made from fruit grown just out beyond the back door. The Göpfrich family came to Sonoma County in the early 1990s, when Ray retired from an academic career teaching dentistry, and, when they learned that the old vineyard on the property was too neglected to save, they planted the Bordeaux- and Rhône-style varietals that thrive in the northern Dry Creek *terroir*. One of the fortunate results of this diverse vineyard is that, although Ray only makes six hundred cases of wine a year, there is an excellent range of things to try at Göpfrich.

There is a zinfandel, of course. It's the signature wine of the Dry Creek Valley. When I visited the winery, the folks gathered around were joking about turning "Ray syrah syrah" into a new ditty, and all the evidence pointed to an enthusiastic appreciation of his syrah *cuvée* blend. A bit more unusually in the valley, Göpfrich also produces a cabernet sauvignon, a consistent gold medal winner in wine competitions, and, as Ray will tell you, because the Dry Creek Valley cabernets are less well known, they are one of the best values in the valley. Ray's estate reds range from $25 to $40.

But before you get to these small-lot reds that have made the Göpfrich reputation, don't be surprised when you are also offered another unique tasting experience. In homage to the family's German roots and to a longstanding friendship with an exchange student who lived with Ray and his wife in younger days, Ray also pours Rheinhessen wines from the Frank Klemmer family vineyards. These imported German whites (under $20)—as with all the wines at Göpfrich, available only in the tasting room or through direct winery sales—are aromatic and floral, and it's a great chance to try just one more family wine that you won't discover anywhere on the grocery store shelves.

HAWLEY WINERY

6387 West Dry Creek Road ✦ Healdsburg

Dry Creek Road, between Lambert Bridge Road

and Yoakim Bridge Road

Tasting *and* winemaker tours daily, by appointment

Tel. 707.431.2705 ✦ www.hawleywine.com

I N THE MIDST OF AN INCREASINGLY COMMERCIALIZED SONOMA WINE COUNTRY, THE DRY CREEK VALLEY IS A BIT OF AN OASIS, and driving along the narrow back lanes here in the northwest corner of the county, with the vineyards and the mustard bloom stretching out for acres before you, it's sometimes hard to keep your eyes on the road. It goes without saying that eyes on the road are a good idea, or maybe a better idea is to find a spot to pull over, take it all in, and talk with one of the families whose passion is for the fruit grown in the heart of this fertile valley.

The Hawley Winery — run by John Hawley and his sons Paul and Austin — is one of these special places. Like so many of the small, fam-

ily operations in the North Bay wine country, visits are by appointment only, and you should not be shy about calling. These are friendly folks. John made his reputation as a winemaker with some of the area's most prestigious commercial estates and was one of the innovators behind the move to barrel fermentation in Sonoma County, and he talks with the easy confidence of expertise about everything from the chemistry of a wine's bouquet to the advantages of sustainable agriculture. The Hawley vineyards are certified organic, and why use pesticides when the local wildlife are content to feast on the wild strawberries and tender weeds that grow underneath the vines? The boys, who grew up in the vineyards and learned their craft the old-fashioned way, are happy to show you first hand what winemaking looks like, and of course to give you a taste of the wines, which are excellent.

The emphasis is on French-style wines made from classic varietals, in the $20 to $30 range, and their 2005 zinfandel (a Dry Creek Valley signature wine) won six different gold medals. With a total estate production of less than four thousand cases a year, however, distribution of the Hawley wines is limited. Art lovers making a visit to Hawley should be sure to ask for a visit to Dana's studio (www.danahawley.com), as well. She paints vibrant and beautiful landscapes of this same valley where her husband and sons spend their days, and one of her creations might just be that perfect souvenir you're looking for.

RAYMOND BURR VINEYARDS AND WINERY

8359 West Dry Creek Road ✦ Healdsburg
Dry Creek Road, between Lambert Bridge Road
and Yoakim Bridge Road
Tasting daily 11AM *to* 5PM
Tel: 888.900.0024 ✦ www.raymondburrvineyards.com

RAYMOND BURR AND ROBERT BENEVIDES MET BACK IN THE 1950s WHEN THEY WERE ACTORS ON THE *PERRY MASON* show, and they went on to work again famously in *Ironsides*. But their most delicious partnership never had anything to do with Hollywood: their love of fine wines and rare orchids has been at the heart of the Raymond Burr Vineyards since they planted their first vines in the late 1980s.

Today, the solar-powered winery is named in memory of Burr, who passed away in 1993, and at the winery Robert Benevides continues to celebrate both their shared passion for this Dry Creek estate and his own family's Portuguese heritage with an active calendar of special events and, of course, with daily tasting opportunities. The Raymond Burr Birthday Bash in late May and the Azores Portuguese Weekend in September are particularly high-spirited affairs. The wines on offer include award-winning chardonnay, cabernet franc, and cabernet sauvignon wines in the $30 to $40 range, and visitors can also sample three different ports made in the classical style, from tinta cão, tinta madeira, and toriga varietals (around $50). Tasting is complimentary.

Whatever you do, don't miss the orchid tour on the estate. It alone is worth the drive to this far end of the Dry Creek Valley. There are more than a thousand stunning varieties in these sultry greenhouses, and the blooms are nearly as intoxicating and fragrant as the wines. Visits are available by advance appointment only on Saturday and Sunday at 11 AM, and it's a rare chance to be introduced to a world-class collection by a renowned expert and devoted enthusiast.

MICHEL-SCHLUMBERGER WINES

4155 Wine Creek Road ✦ Healdsburg
Follow West Dry Creek Road, north *of the* Lambert
Bridge Road, *to* Wine Creek Road.
Tasting *and* estate tours throughout *the* day,
by advance appointment only
Tel: 707.433.7427 ✦ www.michelschlumberger.com

THE MICHEL-SCHLUMBERGER WINERY BEGAN ITS LIFE BACK IN THE 1970s WHEN JEAN-JACQUES MICHEL CAME TO Sonoma County from his native Switzerland and planted fifty acres of vineyards here on the western side of the Dry Creek Valley. The small estate, a partnership between Jean-Jacques and Ridgely Bullock, was simply named Domaine Michel. In the early 1990s, Jacques Schlumberger — whose family has been making wine in the French Alsace, on the west bank of the Rhine River, for nearly four hundred years — joined the enterprise. Michel-Schlumberger Wines was born.

Apart from the excellent pinot blanc you'll find on offer here (a nod to the white wines of eastern France and priced at just over $20), the emphasis at Michel-Schlumberger is on premium Bordeaux-style wines. They make a cabernet sauvignon each year, along with small-lot releases of syrah, pinot noir, merlot, and chardonnay wines, in the $20 to $75 range.

The winery also offers some of the best educational opportunities and special tasting events in the valley, although there is a modest charge.

The traditional tour and tasting package ($15, by appointment only) takes place daily at 11 AM and 2 PM and includes a winemaker tour of the cellars, vineyards, and the Spanish mission–style estate; half the proceeds support special programs in the public schools. You can also arrange vertical tasting appointments if you've always wanted to experience how a wine changes from vintage to vintage ($35), or, during the busy days around the weekend, you can reserve a spot at the noontime

wine and local cheese-tasting extravaganza ($25) or take the Green Tour—an introduction to sustainable and organic farming practices on the estate, which includes a tour of the gardens and wine tasting out in the vineyards. And, if you are wishing you had signed up for a crash course in wines somewhere along the way, there are Thursday seminars on tasting and on the structural components of wine ($75) that will give you a whole new appreciation of what's in that glass in front of you.

MOUNTS FAMILY WINERY

3901 Wine Creek Road ✦ Healdsburg
Follow West Dry Creek Road, north of the Lambert Bridge Road
intersection, to Wine Creek Road.
Tasting by appointment
Tel. 707.292.8148 ✦ www.mountswinery.com

THE MOUNTS FAMILY WINERY IS WHAT BACK LANE WINE TASTING IS ALL ABOUT. You follow the hand-painted sign that reads "Tasting Today" down a gravel track through the vineyards, and there you are on the doorstep of one of the Dry Creek Valley's newest wineries. The family dog is the cellar mascot; the owners, proprietors, and winemakers—Dave and Lana Mounts—live and work on this rural ranch.

Dave grew up in the vineyards, and his family has been growing grapes in Sonoma County for three generations on land that his father bought back in the 1940s. But the winery only got its start in 2005, and they have just celebrated their first release of estate wines. The Mounts craft a select range of small-lot and handcrafted wines, focusing on syrah, petite sirah, zinfandel, and cabernet franc varietals, in the $20 to $30 range, and this is one of the friendliest and most personal wine tasting experiences you'll find anywhere in the county.

A. RAFANELLI VINEYARD AND WINERY

4685 West Dry Creek Road ✦ Healdsburg
West Dry Creek Road, just north *of the*
Lambert Bridge Road intersection
Tasting by appointment
Tel. 707.433.1385 ✦ www.arafanelliwinery.com

THE FOLKS AT A. RAFANELLI VINEYARDS AREN'T ALWAYS GREAT ABOUT RETURNING PHONE CALLS, AND THE TASTING rooms are only open by appointment, but they've been making wines in the Dry Creek Valley for over four generations, and they have one of the best reputations locally for making great red wines. Their zinfandel is generally considered superior and emblematic of the Dry Creek Valley A.V.A. In fact, most of these wines are good enough that there are limits on how many bottles you can buy in the tasting room — which is the only place outside a few high-end restaurants where you'll ever find them. With a total production of just over ten thousand cases a year and this kind of a reputation, you can pretty

well imagine that these wines (most in the $45 and up range) don't come cheap. They've been considered cult wines for years.

But if you do manage to get an appointment — and visitors sometimes can't — it's absolutely worth the trip. The tasting room is up a long steep driveway lined with redwood trees, surrounded by terraced vineyards, and the rustic barn-style winery feels a world away from the glitz and glitter that you'll find in so much of the wine country. This place is still very much a family-run operation, and the tasting appointments are intimate and friendly affairs, with plenty of time to ask questions and find a new favorite. If you do get an appointment, make sure you're not late, because they won't keep your spot. And you can't use your credit card here, so if you plan to buy — and it would be crazy not to take at least one bottle home — be sure to hit the bank machine first (or bring your checkbook).

LAMBERT BRIDGE WINERY

4085 West Dry Creek Road ✦ Healdsburg
West Dry Creek Road, just south *of the* Lambert
Bridge Road intersection
Daily 10:30AM *to* 4:30PM
Tel: 707.431.9600 ✦ www.lambertbridge.com

ITH GREAT WINES AND ONE OF THE MOST CHARMING TASTING ROOMS IN SONOMA COUNTY, LAMBERT BRIDGE Winery is a small family-run production gone snazzy. When I think "wine-country chic," it's Lambert Bridge that comes to mind, and you'll definitely want to charm someone into taking your photo in front of the vintage flatbed truck, stacked with wine barrels, that's parked out front and is still used for special deliveries.

If I were on my honeymoon or on a romantic wine-country weekend, Lambert Bridge would be on my list. The gardens are lovely, and visitors are invited to bring a picnic along and enjoy the surroundings. The winery also offers a dazzling array of special tours and events geared toward wine lovers, including annual harvest tours in September and October, winemaker dinners, and *al fresco* cooking lessons with local chefs throughout the year. You'll drop some serious cash for many of these events (and their reserve room charges a hefty $20 tasting fee, which is double the local average and something many family operations wouldn't dream of asking), but the wines — mostly Bordeaux blends and varietals in the $30 to $40 range — are excellent and highly rated, and you'll get personal service that feels first class all the way.

VINEYARD OF PASTERICK

3491 West Dry Creek Road

West Dry Creek Road, south *of the* Lambert Bridge Road intersection

Tasting daily by appointment

Tel. 707.433.4655 ✦ www.pasterickwine.com

THERE HAVE BEEN GRAPES ON THE SITE OF THE PASTERICK VINEYARDS SINCE THE 1880s, AND THE FARMHOUSE ONCE belonged to the Palmieri family, who established one of Sonoma County's landmarks, the Dry Creek Store. The vineyards today are more recent, planted especially by Gerry Pasterick so he could create his signature California-inflected Côte Rôtie blend. Here on ten steep hillside acres, Gerry—a generous man with a sparkling wit and a passion for *terroir*—grows enough viognier and syrah to produce five hundred cases a year of his complex and eminently quaffable wine. Each year there is just one release ($38), and every bottle is hand-numbered and hand-signed. The afternoon I visited him, he had just finished gluing the labels onto bottles. Pasterick is very much the kind of place where everything about winemaking is intimate and personal.

If you ever wanted a real education in *terroir*, this is the place to come. Gerry will take you out back and show you his two hills. Here in the Dry Creek Valley, the vintners can watch the sun rise over Geyser Peak, and in the far distance you might catch a glimpse of Napa's Mount St. Helena. Three million years ago, both were active volcanoes, and the valley floor is still covered in places with iron-rich ash from prehistoric explosions. You can see it immediately when Gerry points to the pale red of his northern slope. To the south, the hill is brown—the result of 120 million years of crushed bedrock. With a laugh, he'll tell you that his Côte Rôtie style was inevitable: in France, they distinguish between the blond and brown sub-appellations. He's got them both in his backyard, and if you visit at harvest time, you can taste the difference soil makes. It's the same rootstock and the same vineyard practices, but these are different grapes. That is the essence of *terroir*.

The winemaker tour also includes a walk through the stand of coastal redwood trees that run along the back edge of the property amid seasonal waterfalls, and, from there, it's down into the meandering underground caves where the wines are produced and stored. And, of course, you'll taste the wine. It's full of red fruit jam and spices, and it's not something you're going to sample anywhere else.

DE LA MONTANYA ESTATE VINEYARDS AND WINERY

999 Foreman Lane ✦ Healdsburg
From Highway 101, take Westside Road *to* Felta Road,
left *on* Foreman Lane under *the* bridge.
Tasting Friday *to* Sunday 11AM *to* 5PM, Monday *to*
Thursday by appointment
Tel. 707.433.3711 ✦ www.dlmwine.com

THE DE LA MONTANYA FAMILY HAS BEEN WORKING THE LAND IN NORTHERN CALIFORNIA FOR NEARLY TWO HUNDRED years, and, in an era when the true California native is rumored to be an endangered species, they are justifiably proud of having seven generations of local experience behind them. Like so many of the old families in Sonoma, Dennis and Tina De La Montanya also still make a good part of their living selling the grapes grown on their property to the big commercial outfits. However, with 15% of their crop they have recently started making some of the valley's most coveted wines. Getting into the tasting room here takes advance planning. Pretty soon, in fact, there will be a waiting list for joining the wine club. The production is limited to around 4,500 cases a year, and club members buy almost all of it. There are no plans to expand production, and that means that this is cult wine in the making.

If you were going to join one wine club while touring the back lanes of Sonoma, De La Montanya would be a good pick. Not only does the family make an astonishing thirty different wines—many of them medal winners at the Sonoma County Harvest Fair and in the

San Francisco Chronicle competitions—but this is a place where wine club members get unique perks, something more than the standard fifteen or twenty percent case discount. The "Pin-Up Wine" series boasts labels with glamorous images of sexy ladies in tasteful boudoir settings, but these are no L.A. models. Every year, wine club members who want to strut their stuff can enter the Halloween drawing and win the chance to raise a few eyebrows. There are also opportunities to challenge your tax accountant and support the Make a Wish Foundation and the Elizabeth Glaser Foundation with premium charity wines, autographed by big-name rock acts like Journey and Eddie Money. But the good causes and good clean fun never get in the way of making serious wines, with an emphasis on pinot, syrah, and zinfandel varietals in the $20 to $35 range.

MADRONA MANOR

1001 Westside Road ✦ Healdsburg
Follow West Dry Creek Road south, to the intersection
of Westside Road.
Wednesday to Sunday 6PM to 9PM
Tel: 707.433.4231 ✦ www.madronamanor.com

A VICTORIAN-ERA MANSION ON THE NATIONAL HISTORIC REGISTER, SET AMONG VINEYARDS AND SPRAWLING GARDENS, the Madrona Manor makes you understand what traveling first class in the age of the robber barons must have felt like. Situated in one of most luxurious inns in the Dry Creek Valley appellation, the dining room offers pricey but delicious *prix fixe* tasting menus ($75 and up) with a focus on local ingredients and the best of wine-country cuisine. Wine-tasting menus are also offered, or the proprietors are happy to open your bottle for a small fee ($15, limit two). But my favorite time to go is actually mid-afternoon, when the dining room is closed, but if things are quiet you can still order a cheese plate and a bottle of wine and sit in the front parlor playing chess by the fireplace.

DRY CREEK GENERAL STORE

3495 Dry Creek Road ✦ Healdsburg
Dry Creek Road west *from* Highway 101,
located *at the* Lambert Bridge Road intersection.
Monday *to* Thursday 6AM *to* 6PM, Friday *to* Saturday 6AM *to* 7PM
Tel: 707.433.4171 ✦ www.dcgstore.com

FOR A FANCY LUNCH IN THE DRY CREEK VALLEY AREA, YOU'LL NEED TO HEAD BACK TOWARD HEALDSBURG WHERE gourmet pleasures await. But up in this rural far end of the county, many of the wineries have picnic grounds where you can settle in with a deli lunch and a bottle of something special, and the Dry Creek General Store—a landmark in the valley since 1881—is the perfect place to pick up all the fixings. You can order custom sandwiches or just pick up a fresh baguette to enjoy with gourmet cheeses and local olives. If you don't want to open one of your recent finds, you'll also discover a large selection of Dry Creek wines and a shaded beer garden where you can relax over a cold pint. Unless the quirky full-service bar is more your style: it's got a bit of the wild west about it still and is a local favorite. The store is often closed on Sunday.

DRY CREEK PEACH
AND PRODUCE

2179 Yoakim Bridge Road ✦ Healdsburg

Follow either Dry Creek Road *or* West Dry Creek Road
to Yoakim Bridge Road.

July *and* August, most weekends 12PM *to* 5PM (hours vary somewhat)

Tel: 707.433.8121 ✦ www.drycreekpeach.com

A GENERATION OR TWO AGO, BEFORE CALIFORNIA BECAME WINE COUNTRY AND A SMALL RANCH COULD BE SOLD TO aspiring winemakers (and these days, increasingly, to out-of-town investors) for staggering sums of money, prune and peach orchards covered the Dry Creek Valley floor. Today, most of the orchards are gone, and the Dry Creek Peach and Produce stand is the last fruit farm in the area. If you have never tasted a peach warm off the tree in the California sunshine, you haven't ever really tasted a peach at all. Just the smell of them can leave you dizzy.

The fruit at Dry Creek Peach and Produce is grown organically, and this family-run business specializes in selling fruit and homemade jam (along with a small selection of heirloom vegetables) at local farmers markets and to some of the Bay Area's most renowned restaurants. But during most Saturday and Sunday summer afternoons in July and August, from about noon onward, you'll be able to find them at the store or in the orchards. You can stop for a glass of homemade lemonade and buy some of the most exquisite peaches you will find anywhere.

CHAPTER 2

ALEXANDER VALLEY

Named after the nineteenth-century pioneer Cyrus Alexander, the Alexander Valley was once open ranch land. Today, the area is known for producing some of California's finest cabernet sauvignon, and along its back lanes you'll find numerous small family wineries and some of the county's best dining establishments.

The A.V.A. begins just north of Healdsburg, with its tree-lined plaza and boutique shops, and it runs northward along Highway 101 beyond Cloverdale. The most charming wine tasting route is to work your way south from Cloverdale, sampling your way down the River Road, perhaps taking in the historic site of the Italian Swiss Colony in Asti, and picking up Highway 128 — the main wine road of the Alexander Valley — in Geyserville. From the southern end of the appellation, you can continue driving through the Chalk Hill or Knight's Valley areas, where the scenery is lovely but there are few wine tasting opportunities.

SAUSAL VINEYARDS AND WINERY

7370 Highway 128 ✦ Healdsburg

Highway 128, *at the* Pine Flat Road intersection

Tasting daily 10AM *to* 4PM

Tel. 707.433.2285 ✦ www.sausalwinery.com

ROSE AND LEO DEMOSTENE BOUGHT THE 125-ACRE SAUSAL RANCH BACK IN THE 1950s, BUT THE COUPLE ALREADY had generations of winemaking experience behind them. Rose's father started out working at the historic Italian Swiss Colony in Asti, and by the 1920s the family ran the old Soda Rock Winery. Leo was the winemaker. When the couple purchased their own vineyards here in Healdsburg, it was land that had first been planted with zinfandel grapes back in the 1870s. Today, these are some of the oldest vines in all of Sonoma County.

Rose and Leo also planted more grapes, of course, and in 1973 — when their four children founded Sausal — those zinfandel and cabernet sauvignon vines became the backbone of the new winery's sixty acres of estate vineyards. When you arrive at Sausal, there is no missing that this is very much a family-run business. The walls of the tasting room are lined with old black-and-white photographs that show what winemaking in Sonoma County used to be like, before the big developers and commercial outfits all arrived. The atmosphere is friendly and convivial, and, more often than not, strangers at the tasting bar end up swapping stories and then business cards.

It's easy to be cheerful at Sausal. The wines are good, and the prices are surprisingly modest. Although the family makes less than fifteen thousand cases of wine a year—much of it highly rated by major publications such as *Wine Enthusiast*—their wines start in the $10 to $20 range. They are renowned for their old-vine and private reserve zinfandels, but you can also try all estate-grown selections ranging from sangiovese and chenin blanc to Italian-style blends.

ROBERT YOUNG
ESTATE WINERY

4960 Red Winery Road ✦ Geyserville
From Highway 128, turn east *on* Pine Flat Road
and north *on* Red Winery Road.
Tasting daily 10AM *to* 4:30PM
Tel: 707.431.4811 ✦ www.ryew.com

THE YOUNG FAMILY HAS BEEN FARMING THIS PARCEL OF SPRAWLING RANCH LAND ON THE EASTERN SIDE OF THE Alexander Valley since the late 1850s, when Peter Young gave up looking for gold and settled down just outside the small community that would come to be known as Geyserville. Five generations later, the Young family — siblings Fred, Jim, JoAnn, and Susan — still farm this historic ranch, which has been the site of estate vineyards since the 1960s. Today, when you arrive at the winery it feels like you've stumbled across someone's much-loved family home. There's the old ranch house with its long veranda looking right out onto acres upon acres of vineyards that turn brilliant reds and oranges in the autumn after harvest. Over in the big white barn, in the shade of ancient oak trees, you'll find the small tasting room and the friendly staff.

Of course, the wines are excellent. You can't make bad wine as a small proprietor and stay in business this long in Sonoma County. Their signature Bordeaux blend "Scion" is particularly well regarded, and past vintages have been awarded a place on the *Wine Enthusiast*'s Top 100 Wines list. They also produce a wonderfully intense Burgundian-style chardonnay and an estate-grown merlot, both of which continue

to delight the critics. There are smaller plantings in the vineyards of pinot blanc, petit verdot, malbec, white riesling, cabernet franc, viognier, sangiovese, and melon de Bourgogne. The wines range from about $40 to $60, and the $5 tasting fee is refunded with purchase. The estate has some fine caves, which are worth a look, but if you want the winemaker tour you have to be sure to call in advance for an appointment.

WATTLE CREEK WINERY

25510 River Road ✦ Cloverdale
Highway 101 *to* Citrus Fair Drive exit, east *on* First Street,
south *on* River Road
Tasting daily by appointment
Tel. 707.894.5166 ✦ www.wattlecreek.com

HERE IN THE FAR NORTHEASTERN REACHES OF SONOMA COUNTY, THE RUSSIAN RIVER SHAPES THE LANDSCAPE AS it makes its capricious and winding way to the Pacific, and the drive along the River Road offers panoramic views. Those views, however, are nothing compared to the panoramas that await those lucky visitors whose destination is Wattle Creek Winery, set amid a fifty-six-acre vineyard estate that John Paul Getty would be proud to call home.

This place isn't just beautiful. In all of the wine country, nowhere is the welcome more gracious. Wine tasting takes place in the poolside guest cottage, and this relaxed and friendly venue sets the tone perfectly. Everything here is leisurely — no need to elbow your way to a bar and wave your empty glass hopelessly. As you sip the wines and nibble on a plate of gourmet cheeses, you'll really get to talk about the craft of

winemaking and the Wattle Creek philosophy. More likely than not you'll also get a chance to meet the owners Christopher and Kristine Williams, who came to California from their native Australia and named their winery after its national flower, the wattle or acacia. They will tell you that their love of wines began as collectors; curiosity and connoisseurship are the hallmarks at Wattle Creek.

Wattle Creek makes some special wines. The production is 100% estate, with wines made from the grapes grown here and on another six hundred acres just a bit to the north, in Mendocino's Yorkville Highlands, and a good part of the eighteen thousand or so cases they produce each year are given over to their three signature award-winning wines: a sauvignon blanc, a syrah, and a Rhône-style Triple Play blend of syrah, petite sirah, and viognier. Winemaker Michael Scholz, another Australian transplant with six generations of family experience behind

him, also makes some eclectic small-lot wines that are a rare treat, including a red sparkling shiraz ($35) that might just be the perfect wine with your holiday turkey.

Most of the wines at Wattle Creek are in the $25–35 range, and, if you just can't make it all the way up to Cloverdale on your wine-tasting adventure, their San Francisco tasting room is right in the heart of Ghirardelli Square (900 Northpoint Street, Suite E211; tasting daily 11 AM-9 PM, winters until 7:30 PM, tel. 415-359-1206).

GARDEN CREEK RANCH VINEYARD WINERY

2335 Geysers Road ✦ Geyserville
Highway 128 & Geysers Road, 3 miles north of
Alexander Valley Road
Tasting daily by appointment
Tel. 707.433.8345 ✦ www.gardencreekvineyards.com

SOMETIMES IN SONOMA COUNTY, TROLLING ALONG THE BACK LANES, YOU CAN STILL DISCOVER THE NEXT GENERATION of winemaking talent before everyone else does. Unfortunately, the Garden Creek wines almost certainly aren't going to be a secret much longer. Only a few years after releasing their first vintage, Justin Miller and Karin Warnelius-Miller have already garnered national attention from *Wine Enthusiast* and *Savor* magazines. All the

fuss was caused by just a couple hundred cases of their hand-crafted Bordeaux-style red, known as "Tesserae" (around $70). The name comes from the word for the small pieces of broken tile that are used to create a mosaic, and this harmonious combination of elements is the essence of the house philosophy here at Garden Creek. Currently, production is limited to five

hundred cases of this premium cabernet sauvignon blend and to two hundred cases of estate chardonnay.

If Garden Creek is a new enterprise, Justin and Karin come to winemaking with a lifetime of experience. Karin grew up locally, in the middle of vineyards planted with old Italian-style varietals. Justin's family has owned the one hundred acres here on the Garden Creek ranch since the 1950s, and he was running the vineyards at eighteen. The thing you notice on first meeting them is a hands-on style born of experience. A visit to Garden Creek starts with the scents of wisteria and redwood over in the winery. Justin milled the boards for the building. In fact, 50% of the building materials came from reclaimed sources, and it's all solar-powered. It's the same in the vineyards. The couple farms the ranch using organic and biodynamic techniques, composting even the wastewater from the winemaking process and hand-thinning the vineyards during the hot, dry summers in order to achieve maximum quality and consistency.

If this all sounds like a lot of hard work, don't let it give you the wrong idea. This is also one of those places where the natural beauty draws you into its own quiet rhythms. The creek bubbles softly in the background, and in mid-May peonies come tumbling out of the fences. You gather around an old oak barrel by candlelight for a taste of wine and some local gourmet nibbles in the cellars. Back out in the sunlight, there's the long view of the valley and the hillside olive groves, where by special request you can settle in for a winemaker's luncheon and get a hands-on lesson in understanding *terroir* and the Bordeaux style. Tasting fees for special requests vary.

LOCALS

21023 "A" Geyserville Avenue ✦ Geyserville
Exit Highway 101 *at* Geyserville.
Daily 11AM *to* 6PM
Tel. 707.857.4900 ✦ www.tastelocalwines.com

ISHING NOW YOU'D MADE AN APPOINTMENT TO TASTE SOME OF THE HAWLEY FAMILY WINES, BUT ARE THINKING it's too late? Or some of the Ramazzotti wines? Or the local vintage crafted by the Arbios family? Or Ross, McFadden, or Topel? All is not lost. Even this far north, Sonoma County is still the Bay Area, and Locals is the quintessential wine-country cooperative. In fact, it was the first tasting-room cooperative licensed in California, and it's a Sonoma County tradition. Carolyn and her staff pour wines for ten or so of the area's small-lot wineries (most in the $15 to $30 range), and this is the place to come if it's insider knowledge you're after — anything from restaurant recommendations to help contacting one of the families for a winemaker tour.

FIELD STONE WINERY

10075 Highway 128 ✦ Healdsburg
Just north *of the* Highway 128 intersection with Chalk Hill Road
Tasting daily 10AM *to* 5PM
Tel: 707.433.7266 ✦ www.fieldstonewinery.com

OWNED BY THE STATEN FAMILY FOR MORE THAN THIRTY YEARS, FIELD STONE WINERY IS THE KIND OF PLACE THAT inspires loyalty from its local fans. When I was last there, a couple from down the road were picking up a mixed case for their cellar and making an afternoon of it. Given its reputation for producing some of the Alexander Valley's highest quality wines, it's no wonder. Legendary wine critic Robert Parker applauds Field Stone as a consistent producer of one of California's better sauvignon blancs, and their merlot, cabernet sauvignon, and petite sirah wines (most in the $20–35 range) have all been recent gold medal winners. With a wine list that includes Italian and Rhône varietals, along with more familiar grapes, this is also a good place to branch out and experience a California-style sangiovese or the increasingly popular white viognier.

What's best about Field Stone—like so many of the genuinely family-run small wineries of Sonoma County—is its accessibility. Always wanted to do a barrel tasting? As long as you call in advance, the folks at Field Stone would be more than happy to oblige, whatever time of year you are visiting. After all, it only means walking into the front room. Visitors to the winery walk past a room of stacked oak barrels, with the sweet woody aroma, on the way to the tasting room. This is another one of those working wineries, where you can learn about the craft from those who love it best.

HAWKES WINERY

6734 Highway 128 ✦ Healdsburg

East *of* Highway 101, *at the* intersection *of*

Alexander Valley Road *and* Highway 128

Tasting daily 10AM *to* 5PM

Tel: 707.433.4295 ✦ www.hawkeswine.com

I N THE LAST DECADES OF THE NINETEENTH CENTURY, THE ALEXANDER VALLEY WAS ACRE AFTER ACRE OF RUGGED RANCH land, spread out along the small creeks that fill the Russian River to its banks (and sometimes more) come spring. The little stretch of Highway 128 north of Red Winery Road was once known simply as Jimtown, after James Patrick and the general store he ran there. Today, this settlement and the historic Victorian property that remains is home to another small family business, Hawkes Winery, run by Paula and Stephen Hawkes, their son Jake, and their daughter-in-law Laura.

Like so many of the area's small producers, the family worked for decades as growers, supplying high-quality fruit to prestigious premium labels like nearby Silver Oaks, in vineyards they have owned since the early 1970s. The Hawkes have been making wines under their own label for just a few years, and the tasting room only opened in late 2007. While the label is new, the family brings to it two generations of expertise and the passion of those who know and love the land. They make superb small-batch wines, made from 100% estate-grown fruit, with prices in the $25 to $60 range, and if you get chatting at the tasting bar Laura will proudly tell you that they just got their own equipment. Before that, they were crafting their three thousand–odd cases of cabernet sauvignon, merlot, and chardonnay a few miles down the road, at one of the local cooperatives. These are wines worth putting down, and there's still time to discover them before the big-name critics do. Tasting is $5, refunded with a wine purchase, and if you want the private vineyard tour, just give them a call in advance.

PENDLETON ESTATE
VINEYARDS AND WINERY

35100 Highway 128 ✦ Cloverdale

Highway 101 ⁄ Highway 128. The winery is 5 miles north.

Tasting daily by appointment

Tel 707.894.3732 ✦ www.pendletonwines.com

THE OAT VALLEY IS WELL OFF THE BEATEN PATH, AND THE SMALL WINERY THAT MICHALL AND JEANNINE PENDLETON run out of their family home is the last winery in the Alexander Valley appellation before Sonoma County gives way to the cooler, foggier landscape of Mendocino. That means that this isn't the kind of place where you pop in quickly on your way to another couple of appointments in an afternoon. Here, you come to settle in for the kind of one-on-one wine experience that only a passionate small proprietor is going to be able to give you. And it's quite an experience: Driving up through the gates of the Pendleton estates, you find yourself wondering if you've been whisked away to some countryside French château. Except that when you get to the main terrace of the house, perched at the top of a small, narrow valley, you realize that the views are 100% California.

The Pendletons came to the Alexander Valley in the early 1990s with no clear intention of making wines and no family legacy in the industry behind them. Michall still works as a fireman, and Jeannine is a nurse. In fact, Michall credits his passion for winemaking to his friend and mentor David Caffaro, who makes some of the most highly regarded small-lot wines in the Dry Creek Valley. The winemaking here at Pendleton is clearly a labor of love. Michall makes about five hundred cases a year, and all the wines are completely handmade, right down to the month given over to harvesting the grapes on 4.5 acres of estate vineyards.

Despite the small production, there is an impressive array of wines — and an even more impressive array of medals from the wine competitions. The 2005 unfiltered, unfined Russian River zinfandel took a gold at the Sonoma County Harvest Fair. The year after, the petite sirah came away with a gold from a national wine competition. In fact, of the eighteen wines that Michall has entered in contests, every one has earned a medal. Apart from the more familiar cabernet and petite sirah blends, there is an inky Midnite Rosé and Portuguese-style Celebration Cuvée (with seven varietals, including 23% alvarelhão and 20% touriga), both great opportunities to taste something new. Most wines are in the $25 to $45 range, with the opportunity to barrel sample and order futures in the spring, and there is no charge for wine tasting.

Best of all, unlike most wineries in the county, the semi-annual celebrations at Pendleton Estates — a Spring Fling in May and a Harvest Party in October — aren't limited just to members of the wine club. Anyone is welcome to make a reservation, join in the festivities of the crush, take in the views, and get a firsthand introduction to Michall and his wines.

WILLIAM GORDON WINERY

27800 River Road ✦ Cloverdale
Highway 101 *to* Citrus Fair Drive exit,
east *on* First Street, south *on* River Road
Tasting weekends by appointment
Tel: 707.894.2447 ✦ www.williamgordonwinery.com

WHEN YOU GET TALKING TO THE TWO PARTNERS AT WILLIAM GORDON WINERY, WHAT BILL PESONEN AND Gordon Drake tell you is that they don't want to get so big that this isn't fun anymore. This is going to be their retirement after all—Bill from a career as an airline pilot, Gordon from pediatric radiology. Currently, these two neighbors, who made just fifty cases of Hillside cabernet sauvignon (around $45) in 2007, are pretty clearly having a good time—and they are making a great wine.

For their first two commercial vintages, in 2006 and 2007, Bill and Gordon laugh recalling how they took turns crushing the entire lot in a small basket press over in the corner. Like so many of the best boutique vintners in Sonoma County, they started out making garage wines, slowly developing their plantings to match their process, and that means that the spirit here is still a collaborative blue-jeans-and-weekend style. Now that they are planning to add a petite sirah and a zinfandel to their offerings, they've taken the plunge on some larger equipment, but the emphasis at William Gordon is still on handcrafted small-lot wines.

If you've ever wondered what that equipment is or how a winemaker crafts a distinctive wine, this is the place to find out. Tasting takes place in the heart of the production room. Vineyard tours and barrel tasting are available by request. Bill and Gordon also produce an estate olive oil ($20), made from the arbequina and empeltre varietals planted just out behind the winery, which no dedicated gourmet should miss.

LANCASTER ESTATE WINERY

15001 Chalk Hill Road ✦ Healdsburg

Chalk Hill Road, just south of Highway 128

Tasting Monday to Saturday by appointment

Tel: 707.433.8178, ext. 209 ✦ www.lancaster-estate.com

LOCATED AT THE VERY SOUTHERN END OF THE ALEXANDER VALLEY A.V.A. AND SET BACK UP AGAINST THE FOOTHILLS that run to the east of the Russian River, you'll find the little oasis of calm that is the Lancaster Estate Winery. Here, the flowers spill over the garden paths and there are long views of the vineyards from the tasting room door.

Established in the 1990s by Ted and Nicole Simpkins, on the site of former Maacama Creek Winery, this is a family-owned operation with a singular focus: making world-class, small-lot California wines from class Bordeaux varietals. Each year, the couple releases a small selection of estate wines, generally a cabernet sauvignon, a Bordeaux-style *cuvée*, and recently a sauvignon blanc (most in the $40 to $75 range). These are wines widely regarded as collectible and cellar-worthy, and their limited production goes almost entirely to the members of their allocation list.

Newcomers to the Lancaster wines are welcome to come visit the winery, and perhaps you'll want to put your name on the list for an upcoming vintage. Tours include a tasting of their current releases, and you can ask to view the underground caves on the estate. The appointments can be hard to come by, and you often need to call as much as a month in advance, but it's an all-around experience for the senses and a world apart from the crowded tasting bars of the commercial wineries.

ITALIAN SWISS COLONY

DRIVING ALONG THE BACK LANES OF THE WINE COUNTRY, YOU WILL SOON DISCOVER THAT THERE IS NO SHORTAGE of Italian names, and it was many of these same immigrant families that helped the wine industry in California flourish at the end of the nineteenth century. In fact, wine tasting in Sonoma County is nothing new. As early as the 1890s, scenic trains were carrying tourists up from San Francisco for winery tours and picturesque views of the vineyards.

The one place that these early tourists all had on their itinerary was the Italian Swiss Agricultural Colony. Established by Andrea Sbarboro in 1881 in the newly named town of Asti, just south of Cloverdale, the colony was part of the nineteenth-century American progressive vision. Here, unemployed Italian immigrants would be given work in the vineyards at $30 a month wages, plus all the wine a man could drink, and the chance to purchase the land with part of their labor. But the workers were suspicious, and the community was soon converted to a joint-stock company.

By the 1920s that company, the Italian Swiss Colony Winery, had grown to the largest winery in the world and produced Asti's familiar sparkling wines, a range of old-style Italian varietals, and the best-selling "Tipo Chianti," the wine that made those rustic straw-covered bottles popular in America. During the 1960s, following the popularity of the Colony's "Little Old Winemaker, Me" advertising campaign, it had become the most visited tourist attraction in California after Disneyland. This was where the tasting room experience really got its start. Visitors were taken on winemaker tours through the cellars and the vineyards as a prelude to some serious sampling.

The site of the historic vineyards was purchased by Beringer back in the 1980s and has been closed to the public until just recently. In 2008, the landmark winery was reopened as Cellar No. 8 at Asti Winery (26150 Asti Post Office Road, Cloverdale; tours and tasting daily 10 AM-5 PM, tel. 866-557-4970, www.cellarno8.com). The name is a nod to the original cellar, still standing, where the red wines were aged more than a century ago. It's a bit of wine country legend that it would be a shame to miss on your way north.

Curious history buffs can also view the California Historical Landmark for the Italian Swiss Colony at the corner of Asti Road and Asti Post Office Road.

SANTI

21047 Geyserville Avenue ✦ Geyserville
Exit Highway 101 *at* Geyserville.
Serving lunch Wednesday *to* Saturday 11:30AM *to* 2PM;
dinner Monday *to* Saturday 5:30PM *to* 9PM, Sunday 5PM *to* 9PM
Tel: 707.857.1790 ✦ www.tavernasanti.com

SANTI MAKES WHAT IS HANDS-DOWN THE BEST REGIONAL ITALIAN FOOD IN SONOMA COUNTY. WITH THE STIFF competition here in the wine country, that is a bold statement, but once you taste their homemade sausage, you will understand why. I've been known to fly this stuff back to the East Coast in freezer packs, and it's a good part of the reason I have always been a steady regular at the Healdsburg farmers market. You can buy retail from their farm stand—or get them hot off the grill.

As you might expect, the focus at Santi is on meats, charcuterie, and, of course, homemade pasta. The menu is arranged in the traditional order for Italian dining, with antipasti followed by a pasta course and then a meat course. For starters, there is a selection of house-cured salami or a particularly delicious fried artichoke and pecorino salad. The pastas are all handmade and tossed with richly flavored sauces, and the entrées proper range from de-boned chicken to ribeye steak (most entrées $25 to $35, with pastas around $20). But for one of the most convivial dining experiences in Sonoma County, try to make one of their newly announced Italian supper club nights (*prix fixe* $45). These five-course family style dinners are hosted the last Sunday of the month and feature cuisine from the different regions of Italy.

JIMTOWN STORE

6706 Highway 128 ✦ Healdsburg
East *of* Highway 101, *at the* intersection *of*
Alexander Valley Road *and* Highway 128
Open Monday *to* Friday 7AM *to* 5PM, weekends 7:30AM *to* 5PM
Tel. 707.433.1212 ✦ www.jimtown.com

WHILE THE JIMTOWN STORE HAS BEEN A LOCAL LAND-
MARK IN THE ALEXANDER VALLEY SINCE THE 1890s,
when James Patrick started selling provisions to his fellow
pioneers, the place is more than just a Sonoma County
tradition. It's one of the great small American roadside
cafés. And it's hardly undiscovered. You might have read about the place
in the pages of the *New York Times* or *Gourmet*.

For all that, this is still a down-home country place, where you're
just as likely to find the locals swapping the news as out-of-towners
stopping by to pick up the fixings for that quintessential wine country
picnic. You can pre-order box lunches in the morning if your tasting
agenda is particularly busy, or you can just stop by anytime to be
tempted by some delicious home-cooked sweets and steaming good
coffee while you wait.

You'll also find, as you're browsing, a good supply of local wines and
local products, and on the first Thursday of the month, there are special
tasting events in the wine bar, where you can try wines from a rotating
selection of back lane wineries. Best of all for all you last-minute
shoppers, this is the perfect place to pick up a hostess gift for those lucky
enough to have friends driving you around all weekend. There are also

Americana-inspired country toys for the kids back home, wine-country antiques for any of the grownups who are hankering for souvenirs, and the kind of charming vintage atmosphere that makes one wonder if it really wasn't better in the good old days.

HEALDSBURG

Once part of an Indian village set in the midst of an ancient oak and madrone forest, the native Pomo people knew the site of modern Healdsburg as Kale. By the 1840s, this entire area was part of a vast ranch deeded to Captain Henry Delano Fitch. In the 1850s, a settler named Harmon Heald chose his favorite spot in the middle of another man's land, build a rustic squatter's cabin, and set up shop in a little trading post known simply as Heald's Store.

Today, Healdsburg remains true to its early commercial roots. Its shady tree-lined plaza is ringed with some of the wine country's most charming boutique shopping. Café tables and sunny bistros entice you at every turn, and, of course, there are little tasting rooms tucked along side alleys, where you can discover new vintages crafted by talented small proprietors. Healdsburg is also the gateway to the Dry Creek Valley A.V.A. and your best bet for local accommodation or a leisurely lunch. In addition to the excellent restaurants in town, Healdsburg hosts what is arguably the best farmers market in all of Sonoma County on Saturday mornings.

SELBY WINERY

215 Center Street ✦ Healdsburg
From Highway 101, take *the* Central Healdsburg exit.
Tasting room is one block off *the* southeast corner *of the* plaza.
Tasting daily 11AM *to* 5:30PM
Tel. 707.431.1288 ✦ www.selbywinery.com

DOWN ONE OF THE LITTLE SIDE STREETS THAT LEAD OFF THE HEALDSBURG PLAZA YOU CAN FIND THE UNPREPOSSessing tasting room for Selby Winery, set in a little green cottage covered with flowering vines. It's an intimate and friendly setting where you can sample some of Susie Selby's award-winning wines. In the world of women winemakers, she is one of Sonoma County's most talented.

Here in the wine country, the proprietors of small estates usually have one of two stories to tell. Either they come from families that have

grown grapes in Northern California for generations, or they are newcomers who somewhere along the way fell in love with making wine and this luminous little corner of the world and decided to start again. The Selby story is one of the latter. Susie left a career in corporate America to learn the wine business from the

cellar up, and eventually her sister Betsy and brother-in-law Jonathan joined her in the new family business.

Now, fifteen years later, Selby Winery produces on the order of twelve thousand cases a year of Russian River Valley and Sonoma County wine, and there is something here to suit every taste. Her sauvignon blanc recently took a gold medal in the Sonoma County Harvest Fair, and at just around $15 it has to be one of the best bargains in the wine country. It's as good as wines that you'll pay twice as much for. Susie also makes a syrah and a rosé of pinot noir that is wonderfully dry and drinkable, along with an old-vine zinfandel, a pinot noir, and an award-wining merlot that took honors at the 2007 National Women's Wine Competition. If you find yourself at Sundance Resort some year, you'll discover that Robert Redford had the good sense to tap Selby Winery to craft the house chardonnay. The tasting fee is $5, and most wines are in the $15 to $45 range.

STEPHEN AND WALKER, TRUST WINERY LIMITED

243 Healdsburg Avenue ✦ Healdsburg
From Highway 101, take *the* Central Healdsburg exit.
Tasting room is *at the* southwest corner *of the* plaza.
Tasting daily 10AM *to* 6PM
Tel. 707.431.8749 ✦ www.trustwine.com

A PARTNERSHIP BETWEEN TONY STEPHEN AND NANCY WALKER, THE TRUST WINERY LIMITED IS A NEW WINERY with all the bold style of the Wild West, and it won't be an undiscovered secret in the wine country for long. With a tasting room open for less than a year, the place still isn't on most of the free wine maps that you can pick up everywhere in the county. You'd be amazed at how many unadventurous travelers will walk right by anything not on that map, even when it's a welcoming and chic tasting room.

But the folks at Stephen and Walker aren't in a big rush either. The winery is a labor of love for the family members, who dedicate their weekends to the vineyards and — with the help of just one employee, Michael, the tasting room manager — hold down other jobs in the wine industry the rest of the time. They eschew all the commercial trappings of those big-business wineries; this is the kind of place where each bottle is individually numbered and they don't even print bar codes on their bottles. With less than fifteen hundred cases of wine produced a year, and all of it sold directly from the tasting room, what would be the point?

Despite the small-scale operation, there is nothing amateur about the wine that Nancy Walker makes at their production site up in Mendocino. She worked for years as a winemaker at some of the big commercial estates. Trust Winery specializes in premium small-lot wines, made with fruit sourced from vineyards throughout Sonoma, Napa, and Mendocino. Their Dry Creek zinfandel won gold medals at the California State Fair, the Los Angeles International Wine and Spirits Competition, and the Orange County Fair in 2005, and they also make an award-winning pinot noir, a single vineyard designate Howell Mountain (Napa) cabernet sauvignon, a sauvignon blanc, and a vintage port-style dessert wine ($30 to $65 range). With free shipping on your orders, their wine club is also one of the best deals in Sonoma County.

CAMELLIA CELLARS

57 Front Street ✦ Healdsburg
From Highway 101, take the Central Healdsburg exit.
From the plaza, east to First Street, south until
it becomes Front Street.
Tasting daily 11AM to 6PM
Tel. 707.433.1290 ✦ www.camelliacellars.com

THE TASTING ROOMS AT CAMELLIA CELLARS ARE IN AN HISTORIC BRICK WINERY JUST OFF THE CENTRAL SQUARE, just a few blocks down the road from the place where this back lane enterprise got its start—the Italianate Victorian bed and breakfast known as the Camellia Inn, run by Ray Lewand and his daughters. The family started out making wines down in the basement for the enjoyment of their friends and guests. Then, in the mid-1980s, daughter Chris married the University of California at Davis viticulture graduate Bruce Snyder, and opening a small commercial winery here in the heart of Sonoma County seemed like the natural thing to do.

For more than a decade, Chris and Bruce have been producing a small supply of handcrafted wines, including a zinfandel, sangiovese, and cabernet sauvignon, priced in the $25 to $45 range. But their "First Kiss" white wine blend and a rich dolcetto are what the locals enjoy most. The house epigram comes from Eduardo Galeano and sums up what everyone in the wine country already knows: "We are all mortal until the first kiss and the second glass of wine."

SEGHESIO FAMILY VINEYARDS

14730 Grove Street ✦ Healdsburg

From Highway 101, take *the* Dry Creek Road exit east, south *on* Grove
Street; Or, *from the* west side *of the* plaza, follow Healdsburg Avenue
north, west *on* West North Street, north *on* Grove Street.

Tasting daily 10AM *to* 5PM

Tel: 707.433.3579 ✦ www.seghesio.com

THE STORY OF THE SEGHESIO FAMILY IS, IN MANY WAYS, THE
STORY OF WINEMAKING IN SONOMA COUNTY IN MICROCOSM.
This is a fourth-generation Italian family winery, originally
founded in 1895 by Edoardo Seghesio and his young wife,
Angela. Edoardo came to California from his native Piedemonte
and found employment at the historic Italian Swiss Colony up in Asti,
becoming the winemaker and eventually raising enough money to buy

fifty-six acres of ranch land himself in
the northern reaches of the Alexander
Valley. Soon, that ranch land was planted
to zinfandel, and, as the winery grew,
Edoardo acquired another ten acres of
vineyards that were planted to old
Chianti-style field blends. Today, those
fields boast the most ancient sangiovese
plantings in California and rare old-vine
barbera.

By the twentieth century, however,
the Seghesio Family Winery was big

business, and as late as the 1990s the company was producing more than 125,000 cases of wine a year, including their signature zinfandel and Italian blends. Then, fifteen years or so back, the family decided that it was time to consider a new direction. With some of Sonoma County's most storied vineyard holdings, the next generation at Seghesio was determined to give the land its fullest expression and focus on producing premium wines in small, handcrafted lots.

Today, the total production has been limited to thirty thousand cases a year, and the family makes an excellent range of zinfandel wines, as well as a cabernet sauvignon blend, select barbera, pinot grigio, pinot noir, and sangiovese releases, and what is still the wine country's only arneis—crafted from a rare Italian grape perfectly suited to the Sonoma County *terroir*. The wines run from about $20 to $60, and the beautiful roadside tasting rooms feature a bocce ball court and sprawling picnic grounds where you are welcome to contemplate the good life at your leisure.

WILLIAMSON WINES

134 Matheson Street ✦ Healdsburg
From Highway 101, take *the* Central Healdsburg exit.
Tasting room is just off *the* southeast corner *of the* plaza.
Tasting daily 11AM *to* 7PM
Tel: 707.473.0193 ✦ www.williamsonwines.com

THE BEST PART OF EXPLORING THE BACK LANE WINERIES OF SONOMA IS GETTING THE CHANCE TO TALK ONE-ON-ONE with the passionate and talented small proprietors who are living out their dreams in the vineyards and making some great wine. But if that's the best part, second best has got to be finding a wine that is priced at about half of what it should be. These are wineries where, every year, the entire pro-duction sells out, and the only marketing is a classy tasting room and a sign outside the door. At Williamson Wines, this isn't just an accident — it's the house philosophy. When you get chat-ting with Bill Williamson, who runs the family winery along with his wife Dawn, he'll tell you

with a grin that the only people he wants to deal with are the ones who drink his wine. There's no advertising, no distribution, just three thousand cases a year of hand-crafted small-lot wines and a dedication to giving visitors a memorable wine tasting experience.

Bill and Dawn Williamson came to Sonoma County in the early 1990s, but they both grew up in Australia, where Bill spent his summers out in the family vineyards. Bill didn't return to the wine business until later in life, after a successful entrepreneurial career in the software industry that took him from Sydney to California's Silicon Valley. There was never a time, he will assure you, when he didn't love wine. In fact, he saw all the business travel as a great opportunity to train his palate.

It's knowledge he's happy to share: The focus of the tasting experience at Williamson Wines is on finding simple and elegant ways to heighten your enjoyment of wine, from the "fridge food" pairings you'll sample at the tasting bar (all based on gourmet items you're likely to find in the refrigerator after a long day at work) to the half-sized bottles of many wines that they sell. Those splits—priced at just 50% of a full-sized bottle, plus $1—are perfect for nights when you want to have a different wine with every course. For single professionals and business travelers, who can't bear to pour half a bottle of fine wine down the sink the next day, it's a brilliant solution to one of life's perennial frustrations.

The Williamsons make a dizzying array of wines—everything from an easy and approachable Bordeaux-style cabernet sauvignon to chardonnay, pinot noir, shiraz, semillon, and merlot. Every wine they have ever released has won a medal, despite the fact that with a small case production Bill and Dawn prefer not to enter many of the industry's biggest (and more expensive) wine contests. The wines are in the $25 to $75 range, and you can either stop by for a casual tasting at the bar or make an appointment for one of Bill's special dinners, where you'll get the chance to taste the Williamson wines over dinner in the company of a local Michelin-star chef and the winemaker (around $150 per person).

BACAR VINEYARDS

By appointment only

Tel: 707.384.9463 ✦ *Email:* bacarwine@webtv.net

TRACE NUNES IS A ONE-MAN WONDER, AND HE ONLY MAKES ONE WINE — A TRUE *GRAND CRU* BURGUNDY-STYLE PINOT noir that retails for about $100 and is almost exclusively sold to high-end casino steakhouses in Las Vegas. Barring a trip to the city of sin, tasting the Bacar wines involves some advance planning, because Trace is more interested in making his wine than advertising it. At the moment, there's no tasting room and not even a website. The only way to give it a whirl is to make an appointment, and Trace will give you directions out to the vineyards.

If you want to discover something absolutely unique — that exquisite bottle that *none* of your wine-loving friends back home will have heard of — it's worth spending the extra effort. Trace studied under the legendary local winemaker Greg La Follette and is himself a talented young winemaker with a long family tradition in the business. He produces something just over two hundred cases of wine a year, and the grapes are hand-picked and hand-pressed out on the property that he shares with his uncle, who is also a small-production vintner. The vineyards have been in the family since the 1940s. Each bottle at Bacar — the name simply means "wine glass" in Latin — comes signed, and after you meet Trace you'll know that he's put his heart and soul into the bottle, too.

CYRUS RESTAURANT

29 North Street ✦ Healdsburg
From Highway 101, take *the* Central Healdsburg exit.
The restaurant is one block north *of the* plaza.
Dinner daily 5:30PM *to* 9:30PM; bar service 5PM onward
Tel. 707.433.3311 ✦ www.cyrusrestaurant.com

MORE THAN ONE OF THE DEVOTED GOURMETS OF MY ACQUAINTANCE WOULD ARGUE THAT CYRUS IS THE BEST restaurant in Sonoma County. Certainly, that seems to be the emerging critical consensus in the wider world of the culinary press, as well. *Food & Wine* has lauded chef Douglas Keane as the year's best new chef, and his talents have earned Cyrus a place on *Gourmet* magazine's Top 50 Restaurants in America and two Michelin stars. It's the only restaurant in Sonoma County to hold the honor. All this means, of course, that Cyrus is not exactly one of the undiscovered gems of the wine country. It is pretty amazing, though, and sometimes those critics are on to something.

The food is a creative fusion of French and Asian cuisine, with offerings that range from *foie gras* to Thai lobster or local beef loin. The *prix fixe* dinner menu is a remarkably good deal, all things considered, with three- to five-course meals ranging from $75 to $100. The wine list focuses on smaller half-bottles from prestigious French and California estates, allowing you the freedom to try several different wines over the course of the evening. Also worth considering is the Champagne and caviar menu, which might just be the perfect light meal for those very special occasions.

OAKVILLE GROCERY

124 Matheson Street ✦ Healdsburg

From Highway 101, take *the* Central Healdsburg exit.

Located *at the* southeast corner *of the* plaza

Daily 8AM *to* 6PM

Tel. 707.433.3200 ✦ www.oakvillegrocery.com

JUST OFF THE HEALDSBURG PLAZA THERE IS ALSO ANOTHER LOCAL FAVORITE THAT IT WOULD BE FOOLISH TO PRETEND is an undiscovered secret. But when all you want is a gourmet sandwich for lunch or some fixings for an impromptu picnic, the Oakville Grocery is the obvious place to stop. The proprietors have gathered together all that is rare and delicious in Sonoma County on the store shelves, and you can find everything from cured olives to local cheeses and charcuterie at the gleaming glass-cased deli counter. There's a shaded patio out front where you can enjoy hot sandwiches made to order (around $10), or you can order picnic box lunches in advance if you prefer not to build your own.

DOWNTOWN BAKERY AND CREAMERY

308 A Center Street ✦ Healdsburg
From Highway 101, take *the* Central Healdsburg exit.
Located *on the* east side *of the* plaza
Weekdays 6AM *to* 5:30PM, Saturday 7AM *to* 5:30PM,
Sunday 7AM *to* 4PM
Tel: 707.431.2719 ✦ www.downtownbakery.net

O N SATURDAY MORNINGS IN THE SUMMER, WANDERING THROUGH THE HEALDSBURG FARMERS MARKET — WHERE local chefs give cooking demonstrations and the fresh flowers come falling out of the stalls in fragrant waves of color — is the quintessential wine country experience. The only thing that could possibly make it better is a creamy cappuccino and some truly delicious little breakfast pastry to enjoy while you are walking. My weekend ritual always involves a stop at the Downtown Bakery and Creamery. They make fresh breads every morning from locally milled flours, croissants from Sonoma County butter, and a dizzying array of homemade pastries that are often still warm from the ovens. In the afternoons, this is also the place to pick up a baguette for your picnic lunch, a fancy fruit tart for that dinner at a friend's house, or some homemade ice cream just to keep you going, and there is always steaming tea or coffee on offer.

RESTAURANT MIREPOIX

275 Windsor River Road ✦ Windsor
From Highway 101, exit Windsor River Road west.
Tuesday to Saturday 11:30AM to 9PM
Tel. 707.838.0162 ✦ www.restaurantmirepoix.com

JUST SOUTH OF HEALDSBURG OFF HIGHWAY 101 YOU'LL SEE SIGNS POSTED FOR THE LITTLE TOWN OF WINDSOR, which has largely escaped all the commercialization of the wine country. Not far off this beaten path is Restaurant Mirepoix, run by the husband-and-wife team of Matthew and Bryan Bousquet. The French country dining room is calm and intimate, and the cuisine reflects this same signature style. This is classic French bistro dining at its best, with rotating daily specials that range from duck and *coq au vin* to local fish or short ribs. There are also homemade pasta dishes and a selection of different variations on the *steak frites* theme, with most entrées running from $15 to $25. But at under $30, it's the three-course *prix fixe* menu that ranks as one of the best bargains in Sonoma County.

CHAPTER 4

RUSSIAN RIVER VALLEY AND SANTA ROSA AREA

The Russian River Valley A.V.A. rolls out to the west of Highway 101 along the stretch of road that runs from Santa Rosa to Healdsburg, and it takes its name from the powerful river that eventually makes its way to the sea over on the Sonoma coast. During the 1920s and 1930s, small towns along the river flourished as summer vacation resorts for the San Francisco elite, and before that woodsmen and loggers harvested the area's redwood forests for the timber that helped to build the American West. Today, homeowners struggle in the springtime to keep the river from flooding their canyon homes and the small, winding roads that run along the valley floor.

For tourists, the Russian River Valley — in fact, the entire region of Sonoma known to locals simply as the west county — is a magical place, where you can find ancient redwood forests, little towns that time forgot, breathtaking scenery, and, of course, excellent wine tasting opportunities. This cool climate A.V.A., which includes the small sub-appellation known as the Green Valley, is renowned for its chardonnay, pinot noir, and sparkling wines, although other varietals do well in its versatile climate.

Although the area is crisscrossed with dozens of small roads (and you do want to pick up one of those free maps they give out at all the wineries), there are two main wine tasting circuits through the Russian River Valley. Take either the Guerneville Road exit west from Highway 101, which will let you pick up Highway 116 in either direction, or follow the River Road exit west from Highway 101, which will take you along the flood plains right into the heart of the little town of Guerneville (pronounced "Gurnville"). From here, you can take a walk in the redwood forests that are part of the state's Armstrong Preserve. Or if you want to get lunch in one of the two cutest villages in all of California, you can head south on Highway 116 following the signs to Graton (pronounced "Grayton") or, further on, to Occidental. From Occidental, if you can't turn back without dipping your toes in the ocean, now just ten-odd miles away, ask one of the locals how to find the Coleman Valley Road. It twists and turns and winds, and then it leads you, magnificently, over a long bluff to panoramic views of the Pacific.

LYNMAR ESTATE

3909 Frei Road ✦ Sebastopol
Take Guerneville Road *to* Frei Road.
Tasting daily 10AM *to* 5PM; estate visits by appointment
Tel: 707.829.3374 ✦ www.lynmarwinery.com

WHEN YOU ARRIVE AT THE FORTY-TWO-ACRE HOME OF LYNMAR ESTATE, THERE IS A MEDITATIVE SILENCE, and it's not just the scenery that creates this sense of reverence. Although the gardens are a fine example of how serene and verdant a natural dry-climate garden can be, the architecture steals the show. The modern tasting room is a subtle oasis of glass and stone, and at Lynmar everything is about clearing the palate — and the mind — in preparation for a serious wine experience. There is no gift shop and no country clutter. Tasting here happens in gleaming black leather armchairs, in front of the roaring fireplace or over by the vast windows, where the views are just another small luxury. Visitors are served a flight of four wines tableside (in Riedel glasses, of course), and the staff — who are wonders of quiet professionalism — are more than happy to answer any questions about the Lynmar philosophy.

And there is a philosophy. The commitment is to hand-harvested fruit and expressing the potential of *terroir*. The winery is in the process of experimenting with biodynamic and organic growing practices, and total production is still less than fifteen thousand cases a year. Above all, the emphasis is on perfecting just two main varietals: pinot noir and chardonnay. The pinot noir is easily one of the two or three best pro-

duced in the entire appellation, which explains why it has been on the menu at White House functions more than once. It's no surprise that these wines don't come cheap (most in the $35 to $70 range). Tasting fees run from $10 to $25, depending on which wines you're interested in sampling, and the estate visits (which include wine and food pairings and a tour of the estate gardens) are between $45 and $65, but it's worth it. When the back lanes are getting a bit too dusty for you, Lynmar is the perfect retreat for the senses.

PELLEGRINI FAMILY VINEYARDS

4055 West Olivet Road ✦ Santa Rosa
Take Guerneville Road *to* West Olivet Road.
Tasting daily 10:30AM *to* 4:30PM
Tel. 800.891.0244 ✦ www.pellegrinisonoma.com

WHEN THE *SAN FRANCISCO CHRONICLE* NAMED THE TOP FIVE WINEMAKERS OF 2007, ROBERT PELLEGRINI was on the list. For those who know the family and their long history as winemakers in Sonoma, it's no mystery why. When Prohibition drove most small family wineries out of business in the early decades of the last century, limiting production to a mere two hundred gallons for personal use, the Pellegrinis made the most of this small loophole. If they couldn't sell wine, they could sell grapes. For decades, the family made their way as important brokers —first of grapes and, later, once again of wines. Handsome Italian men and their smiling wives, with that fresh-scrubbed look of the 1930s and 40s, stare out of the old family photographs that adorn the walls of the family's tasting room, now run by the third generation of Pellegrini winemakers.

The tasting room is in the middle

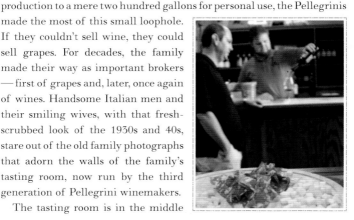

of the action. This is a working winery. The lane back to the buildings is narrow and runs through the sixty-five-acre Olivet Lane vineyards that produce the family's flagship Russian River Valley pinot noir ($35). Their award-winning 2004 merlot — named one of the top 100 wines of 2007 — is grown further north, on property up in the Alexander Valley. The tasting room is filled with row after row of aging barrels, stacked ceiling high, and much of the production takes place out back. (If you call in advance, they'll do their best to arrange a private winemaker tour.) At something over twenty-five thousand cases a year, they are just under the boutique threshold, and you won't be the first person to discover the Pellegrini wines, but there's a reason why they are the darlings of the critics. Tastings are complimentary.

HARVEST MOON ESTATE AND WINERY

2192 Olivet Road ✦ Santa Rosa
Take Guerneville Road to Olivet Road.
Tasting daily 10:30AM to 5PM
Tel: 707.573.8711 ✦ www.harvestmoonwinery.com

RANDY PITTS GREW UP IN A GRAPE-GROWING FAMILY HERE IN THE RUSSIAN RIVER VALLEY, WHERE HIS FOLKS HAVE owned vineyards and ranch lands since the 1970s. His story is a familiar one in Sonoma County: a barrel of garage wine made from some grapes out back that was just too good not to produce commercially. In Randy's case, the wine was zinfandel, and that's still the focus of this new small-production winery.

However, it's the gewürztraminer fans who will want to put the Harvest Moon Winery right at the top of their must-see list. Not only does Randy make a bone-dry Russian River gewürztraminer, but he also handcrafted a small amount of sparkling estate gewürztraminer that is something to experience. You can also find some small-lot pinot noir made from fruit grown in vineyards just down the road. The wines are in the $20 to $35 range, and if you're lucky you might arrive on one of those afternoons when Randy has the outdoor bread oven fired up. You can sample local olive oils, munch some warm bread, and try the wines far from all the rattle and hum of the regular tourist trail.

Harvest Moon also hosts regular events for Wine Country Classrooms (www.winecountryclassrooms.com), where you can register for intensive wine and olive oil tasting seminars ($20 to $80) at various sites throughout the county.

SUNCÉ WINERY

1839 Olivet Road ✦ Santa Rosa

Take Guerneville Road to Olivet Road.

Tasting daily 10:30AM to 5:00PM

Tel: 707.526.9463 ✦ www.suncewinery.com

RRIVING AT SUNCÉ, THERE'S NO MISSING THAT THIS IS A FAMILY BUSINESS. THE ENTRANCE IS A DRIVEWAY, AND THE tasting room is a charming garage conversion, painted in the cheerful and welcoming hues that might serve as a metaphor for the Suncé experience. In front of the house, the roses spill out of the garden. In the back and off to the sides are the vineyards: all three acres of them. The winery is a quintessential family affair, run by the husband-and-wife team of Frane and Janae Franicevic, fourth-generation winemakers from Croatia. These generations of experience along the shores of the Adriatic Sea show in the wines they make.

Along with the perennial Sonoma County favorites—the cabernets, zinfandels, and pinot noirs that have made the region famous—at Suncé you'll also find some unusual varietals. Their 2004 nebbiolo ($50)—made with 100% of what the Italians usually think of as a blending grape—won four gold medals. The only way to get a bottle is to visit the tasting room, but the family has still had to impose a one-bottle maximum to prevent it from disappearing into the cellars. They also make a 50-50 malbec and barbera blend and an award-winning petite sirah, both of which are worth the trip. For folks who like their white wines with just a hint of American oak, there's a nice Burgundy-style chardonnay. And if you're looking for a good reason to open a

bottle, they also release select wines under a second charity label, One World Wine for AIDS, with 25% of the proceeds going to nonprofit AIDS organizations (www.wineforaids.org).

Their small-lot single vineyard designate wines are in the $20 to $50 range, and if you call ahead for an appointment Frane will give you the winemaker tour or let you do some barrel tasting. Or better yet, join the wine club in advance and plan your trip accordingly, because at Suncé the club members do the bottling. For your labors, you get a free case of wine, an amazing 50% off tasting-room sales, and a once-in-a-lifetime wine country experience—unless you come back next year, too.

ROBERT RUE VINEYARD

1406 Wood Road ✦ Fulton

From River Road, head south *on* Fulton Road

to the Wood Road intersection.

Tasting daily by appointment

Tel: 707.578.1601 ✦ www.robertruevineyard.com

THE ROBERT RUE VINEYARD IS THE KIND OF PLACE YOU FIND BY ACCIDENT IF YOU MAKE A WRONG TURN SOME-where. There aren't any signs to even tell you there's a winery out this way. But if you follow a small residential lane, up past the old ranch houses and fields, you will know it's the right place when you see some small vineyards and a little turn-of-the-century American gothic farmhouse with sprawling flower gardens. This is the home of Robert and Carlene Rue, who have farmed these ten acres as grape growers for thirty years. They bought the property as a young married couple back in the early 1970s, and Carlene will tell you with a chuckle that back then they didn't know anything about winemaking. Bob learned from the old man who sold them land everything he needed to know about how to care for these head-pruned and historic vineyards — planted back in the last years of the nineteenth century with old field blends like petite sirah, alicante bouschet, carignane, and mostly zinfandel. It is one of the few vineyards of its sort to have survived the periodic phylloxera outbreaks in the county's history.

When their long-term growing contracts ended in 2000, Robert and Carlene, who run the company with their daughters and sons-in-law, decided the time had come to do more than make some family wines in the garage. They brought on board winemaker Carol Shelton, known locally as the Queen of Zins, and, since their first release, the Robert Rue Vineyards reserve zinfandel (around $35)—the only wine they produce—has risen to the top of the competitions. In less than a decade, the wine has been awarded nineteen gold medals.

The total production at Robert Rue is under one thousand cases of wine a year, and they are looking forward to opening a new tasting room in the winery that they are building out back. But for now, everything starts at Carlene's kitchen table, where like any friend of the family you are offered a complimentary glass of the house wine and some cheese and crackers. She knows all the members of the wine club personally, and as you get chatting you'll soon understand why. After, Bob will take you out for a tour of the vineyards, where the kids can let off some steam (but no dogs, please), and he'll tell you about the local *terroir*—how the evening fogs roll in from the Pacific so the grapes ripen slowly and how the hard pan in the soil makes the vines struggle just enough to produce a hearty wine with rich tannins. So bring your sturdy shoes and all your questions. This is back lane wine tasting at its most intimate and most pleasurable.

IRON HORSE VINEYARDS

9786 Ross Station Road ✦ Sebastopol
Take Guerneville Road west to Gravenstein
Highway/Route 116 north, then west to Ross Station Road.
Tasting daily 10AM to 3:30PM; estate tours by
appointment Monday to Friday at 10AM
Tel. 707.887.1507 ✦ www.ironhorsevineyards.com

PERCHED HIGH OVER THE VALLEY FLOOR, WITH LONG VIEWS OF THE VINEYARDS AND OAK COVERED HILLS, IRON HORSE Vineyards is a hilltop oasis, complete with swaying palm trees. Owned and operated by the Sterling family, Iron Horse also makes what is easily one of the two or three best sparkling wines in all of California, and they are leading the way in the establishment of the Green Valley A.V.A. as a premium locale for wines made in the *méthode champeneoise*. In 2007, when the *San Francisco Chronicle* rated the Best of the West, three of their wines — two vintages of bubbly and a Green Valley chardonnay — were among the top 100.

The loamy soil of the Green Valley and the cooler climate here in the west county produces fruit with the higher acid and delicate mineral quality that is perfect for sparkling wines. In fact, this is bubbly that can compete on the world stage. Iron Horse Vineyards made its

name as a small producer in the 1980s when the Reagan White House asked the winery to produce a special Russian Cuvée for the summit meetings with Gorbachev. The wine, of course, was a hit, and the family still jokes that they deserve total credit for ending the Cold War. The Russians prefer their bubbly just a little bit sweeter, so the wine is a sweet-style *brut*. There are also dry *brut* and *brut rosé* offerings. Best of all, as the dollar plunges, could there be a better moment for discovering excellent domestic sparkling wine? The Iron Horse bubbly starts at around $35 and their high-end *tête de cuvée* caps out at around $80.

While Iron Horse Vineyards is worth the visit above all for the views and the sparkling wines, they also produce a range of still wines — primarily pinot noir and chardonnay — that will give curious wine adventurers a good sense of what is unique about vintages crafted here in the Green Valley. Still wines range from about $20 to $75, but most are in the $30 range, and, because Iron Horse is one of the larger boutique producers (around thirty thousand cases a year), these are wines you sometimes can find back home if you discover a new favorite. The tasting fee is $10 for the regular release wines and $15 for the reserve wines, which you can sample in the fresh air, gathered around an outdoor tasting bar overlooking the vineyards.

MARTINELLI VINEYARDS AND WINERY

3360 River Road ✦ Windsor

From Highway 101, exit River Road west.

Tasting daily 10AM to 5PM

Tel. 707.525.0570 ✦ www.martinelliwinery.com

THE MARTINELLI FAMILY HAS BEEN FARMING IN THE WINE COUNTRY SINCE THE 1860s, WHEN GIUSEPPE AND LUISA Martinelli came to California from their native Tuscany. By 1899, the couple had saved just enough money to buy a small tract of land on a steep hillside, where they planted their first vineyards with rootstock that they had brought with them from Italy. Working the 60-degree angle of the field was so laborious and challenging that it soon became known simply as the Jackass Hill, and today this century-old vineyard is the steepest non-terraced slope in Sonoma County — and home to some of the region's best single vineyard designate zinfandel.

Most of the wines at Martinelli are single vineyard designate, in fact, and today the estate winery is owned and operated by Lee Martinelli and his sons Lee Jr. and George, now the fifth generation of family winemakers. The tasting rooms are set just off the River Road in charming historic hop barns, where much of the production still takes place on site. True to their roots as growers and farmers, the family still sells 90% of the fruit grown on the properties to other vintners, but that other 10% is left in the hands of their neighbor and one of the county's most talented winemakers — Helen Turley, who won the coveted Winemaker of the Year award from *Food & Wine* in 1999 and continues to make some of the finest wines in California.

The total case production at Martinelli is under twelve thousand, and the wines range from Sonoma Coast chardonnays to classic Russian River pinot noir, zinfandel, and sauvignon blanc wines. There are also some more unusual offerings, including a dry gewürztraminer and a muscat alexandria made from the old head-pruned vines planted on Jackass Hill in the very beginning. Most wines are in the $30 to $60 range, and they are a perennial favorite with serious collectors. And it's no wonder; since 2006, Martinelli has had nine wines rated over 90 points by trendsetting guru Robert Parker.

DUTTON-GOLDFIELD WINERY

5700 Occidental Road ✦ Santa Rosa
From Highway 101, exit Guerneville Road west,
turn south *on* Fulton Road *and* west on Occidental Road.
Tasting daily 10AM *to* 4PM
Tel. 707.568.2455 ✦ www.duttongoldfield.com

APARTNERSHIP BETWEEN STEVE DUTTON AND DAN GOLD-FIELD, THE DUTTON-GOLDFIELD WINERY WAS FOUNDED in 1998 as a collaboration between one of the west county's oldest farming families and one of Sonoma County's most innovative cool-climate winemakers. Steve grew up tending the grapes on his father's Russian River vineyards. Dan studied enology at the University of California at Davis back in the 1980s and went on to work his magic with pinot noir as the winemaker at La Crema. The result over the past decade has been a winery known for producing some of Russian River's most distinctive and celebrated wines, primarily excellent chardonnay and pinot noir wines with smaller releases of zinfandel and syrah. *Wine & Spirits* has ranked Dutton-Goldfield as one of the 100 Top Wineries of the Year for four years running, and you'll find a friendly welcome at the low-key tasting room they share with Balletto Vineyards.

BALLETTO VINEYARDS

5700 Occidental Road ✦ Santa Rosa
From Highway 101, exit Guerneville Road west, turn south
on Fulton Road *and* west *on* Occidental Road.
Tasting daily 10AM *to* 4PM
Tel: 707.568.2455 ✦ www.ballettovineyards.com

SHARING A ROADSIDE TASTING ROOM WITH THE DUTTON-GOLDFIELD WINERY JUST TO THE WEST OF SANTA ROSA, Balletto Vineyards is a small family estate that produces some of the best-priced wines in the Russian River Valley, including the pinot noir and chardonnay wines that are the signature of the A.V.A. Here, you'll also find some other wines that are perfect for a long afternoon out on the deck: a crisp pinot gris, a spicy gewürztraminer, and even a rosé of pinot noir that the *San Francisco Chronicle* ranked as one of the Top 100 Wines of 2007. Most wines are in the $15 to $25 range.

The wines are, of course, estate grown and made from fruit that is still picked and sorted by hand. That's what you would expect from a family that has its roots in

farming here in Sonoma County. The winery is owned and operated by John Balletto and his wife Terri, who started out growing vegetables on the Russian River ranch property that today is planted with acres of estate vineyards.

SIDURI WINES

980 Airway Court, Suite C ✦ Santa Rosa
From Highway 101, exit Bicentennial Way West, turn
north *on* Range Road, west *on* Piner Road, *and*
north *on* Airway Drive *to* Airway Court.
Tasting daily by appointment
Tel: 707.578.3882 ✦ www.siduri.com

ADAM AND DIANNA LEE WILL TELL YOU THAT THEY FELL IN LOVE DRINKING WINE BACK IN THEIR NATIVE TEXAS, WHERE Adam worked in wine sales and Dianna in gourmet foods. They visited the North Bay wine country as part of that romance, and they made their first four barrels of pinot noir in the early 1990s from grapes they bought in the newspaper classifieds. That year Adam was 28, and Dianna was just 23, but they had already immersed themselves in winemaking, scouring books for information on the technical aspects of the craft and learning first hand by working for some of the area's other small wineries.

The story of what happened next is the stuff of legend. That summer Adam and Dianna managed an acre of vineyards they had secured under contract, dropping most of the fruit to get intense flavors, and got lucky that year with natural fermentation and the native yeasts. The result was what they knew was a great wine — and, when they heard that the celebrated wine critic Robert Parker was staying at a nearby hotel, they boldly dropped him off a bottle. The result was their first great rating and the beginning of their reputation for making some of the country's best pinot noir.

Today, Adam and Dianna still focus on making about ten thousand cases a year of premium pinot noir wines, most in the $25 to $50 range, released unfiltered and unfined and made from fruit grown in vineyards as far north as Oregon and as far south as Santa Barbara. Recently they have also started up a partnership in a second winery with Dianna's family, and visitors can also sample the Novy Family Wines — mostly syrah, zinfandel, and chardonnay. The emphasis in the tasting room is on good wines and not glitz, so when you visit expect to find yourself experiencing a working winery in action. Here on the production site, barrel tasting is easy. If you become one of their direct mail customers and can't make it back to Sonoma every spring to try the new vintage, Adam and Dianna travel regularly hand-selling their family wines and always try to arrange special wine tasting events in the cities they visit. It's the only wine "club" you'll find where the winemakers come to you.

TARA BELLA WINERY
AND VINEYARDS

3701 Viking Road ✦ Santa Rosa
From River Road west, turn south *on* Olivet Road,
then east *on* Viking Road.
Tasting daily by appointment
Tel: 707.544.9049 ✦ www.tarabellawinery.com

I F YOU FIND YOURSELF IN THE WINE COUNTRY DURING THE CRUSH, YOU WILL QUICKLY DISCOVER THAT THERE ARE PARTIES and special events galore but few opportunities to experience the harvest first hand. For most winemakers, these few short weeks are the culmination of a year's work, and especially at the larger vineyards time is just too precious. But for curious wine enthusiasts, this can be the perfect moment to strike out for some of the smallest back lane wineries, and if you had to choose just one place to be during the crush, it might well be the Tara Bella Winery and Vineyards. Here, Rich and Tara Minnick work six acres of vineyards, and they make just one wine: less than five hundred cases of an entirely estate grown and hand-tended, ultra-premium cabernet sauvignon (around $65).

Because Rich and Tara take the "bud to bottle" approach to winemaking, the pace is slower on this small home estate. Everything here is about quality over quantity. The Russian River A.V.A. is best known for its pinot noir wines, but it is also excellent *terroir* for cabernet sauvignon, provided a vintner is prepared to drop a good deal of the fruit early in the season. Cabernet grapes need just that little bit of extra sunshine and breathing room to ripen fully here in the valley. It's all

about the pursuit of perfection come harvest time, as well. It takes Rich and Tara a full month to pick the vineyards because they hand harvest each row of grapes, only taking fruit at the ideal sugar concentrations. Because nothing is hurried here, it is one of the few places where visitors are welcome even during the crush.

The result is a remarkably consistent fruit-forward, low-alcohol wine that has won medals year after year. In less than a decade, the Tara Bella cabernet has taken thirteen gold medals, which includes two coveted double golds. Distribution is only through the tasting room or mail order direct sales, and they sell out every year. A while back, the wine was even featured on CNN's evening news, and if you want a sneak preview of the Tara Bella experience you can watch the video clip on their website. Better yet, just make an appointment and be prepared for a pleasant surprise. Down at the end of narrow gravel lane, you find Rich and Tara's wine country retreat, a stucco home-turned-winery surrounded by palm trees and vineyards. Rich will take you down into the cellars for a barrel tasting and then it's off for a walk through the vineyards in some of the most congenial company you'll find anywhere in the county. After, of course, you'll head up to the tasting room, where you'll sample the wine and perhaps pick up a bottle or two as a special treat for some blustery winter night back home. Either way, there's no charge for the visit, and it's the kind of experience that you are only going to find off the beaten track.

BATTAGLINI ESTATE WINERY

2948 Piner Road ✦ Santa Rosa

From Guerneville Road, head north *on* Fulton Road,

then west *on* Piner Road.

Tasting daily by appointment

Tel: 707.578.4091 ✦ www.battagliniwines.com

IUSEPPE "JOE" BATTAGLINI CAME TO THE UNITED STATES IN 1956 FROM HIS NATIVE LUCCA, AND THE VINEYARDS HERE —planted in 1885 by the Lagomarsino family with zinfandel and petite sirah grapes—are also part of Sonoma County's Italian winemaking tradition. Joe and wife Lucia bought this twenty-five-acre estate in 1988, and founded a family winery in the midst of these historic vineyards. Their first vintage was in 1994, with 250 cases of wine. Today the total production is just over two thousand cases. And, as you might expect, this is wine crafted in the old-style Tuscan way. The grapes are dry farmed and allowed to struggle and ripen beautifully without artificial irrigation. The vines are head pruned, and the grapes are hand picked.

It's not just that you'll find traditional Italian-style wines at the Battaglini Estate Winery: When you drive in, you feel like you are in Italy. During the barrel tasting weekend, Italian love songs are blaring from the small barn turned tasting room, where there are posters of Rome and Lucca on the walls, with little flags showing the streets where Joe's family still lives. If you ask about his home town, from behind the counter, he'll bring out a picture book and show you the sites, maybe even share with you his best picks for restaurants in this small town or

one of his favorite recipes. Even on a busy day Joe and his family make sure everyone feels a part of the tasting experience. His sons are pouring barrel tastes out front, and it's all in good spirits. From the courtyard, you can see the shaded arbor where the family dinners must be held, at the house just next to the tasting room, with the vineyards beyond.

Most years the Battaglini wine club does a trip to Lucca, led by the family, and you know it must be an amazing experience, but if you can't get to Italy, here's the alternative. For the price of a week in Tuscany, you can haul home a lot of wine. Battaglini's is a piece of the old country, a place filled with conviviality and great wine. Their zinfandels have been consistent medal winners at the state harvest fairs and in national competitions, and they also produce excellent petite sirah, chardonnay, and late harvest chardonnay wines, priced in the $15 to $50 range. You can buy futures by the case at a significant discount, and during their autumn Stomp Event fledgling winemakers can try their hands (or feet) at crushing grapes the old-fashioned way.

WOODENHEAD WINE

5700 River Road ✦ Santa Rosa

Take Highway 101 *to* River Road. The winery is

west *of the* Olivet Road intersection

Tasting Thursday *to* Sunday 10:30AM *to* 4:30PM

Tel: 707.887.2703 ✦ www.woodenheadwine.com

THE EDITORS AT *FOOD & WINE* HAVE FALLEN IN LOVE WITH THE WOODENHEAD PINOT NOIR WINES, FEATURING THEM now two years running in its glossy pages, and it's easy to see why. Made with fruit sourced from Sonoma, Mendocino, and Humboldt Counties, winemaker Nikolai Stez (a long-time veteran of the cult team at the allocation-only Williams Selyem Winery) and partner Zina Bower specialize in premium single vineyard designate pinot noir and zinfandel wines ($30 to $45 range).

The Woodenhead tasting rooms are perched on a hillside overlooking the Russian River Valley floor, and you'll want to take in the views from the deck for sure. But first, head to the bar, where the ambiance is warm and rich and most days you can sample excellent handcrafted wines in surprising peace and quiet.

ARMSTRONG REDWOODS
STATE RESERVE

17000 Armstrong Woods Road ✦ Guerneville
Follow River Road to Guerneville, turn north
on Armstrong Woods Road.
Daily 8AM until one hour after sunset;
visitor center daily 11AM to 3PM
Tel 707.869.2015 ✦ www.parks.ca.gov/parkindex

FIRST SET ASIDE AS A NATURE PRESERVE DURING THE 1870s BY LOGGER AND LANDOWNER COLONEL JAMES Armstrong, this state reserve is one of the last remaining vestiges of the great coastal redwood forests that once covered the Russian River Valley. It is a seven hundred–acre old growth grove that feels untouched by the millennia. In fact, there are trees here that have stood for many centuries, including the fourteen hundred-year-old Colonel Armstrong tree. If you have never stood in a redwood grove and experienced the monumental silence that comes with woods this ancient and towering, it would be a pity to miss your chance now. You don't need hiking boots or heavy outdoor gear, just a warm sweater and some sensible shoes. There are plenty of easy walks through the preserve, and if you come first thing in the morning, when the fog is still creeping through the valley, you won't have to miss a minute of wine tasting either. A daily pass is $6 per vehicle, with no charge for pedestrians or bicyclists.

SANTA ROSA

Located in the heart of Sonoma County, where Sonoma Highway (12) meets Highway 101, Santa Rosa is an easy drive from many of the county's most famous appellations, including the Russian River Valley and Sonoma Mountain. While not as quaint or adorable as some of the smaller towns in the area, Santa Rosa is where the locals go when they want world-class food at real-world prices. The city boasts some of the finest small restaurants in the wine country — and some of the best bargains.

DIERK'S PARKSIDE CAFÉ

404 Santa Rosa Avenue ✦ Santa Rosa
Breakfast *and* lunch daily; Purveyor's Dinner
last Friday *of the* month
Tel: 707.573.5955 ✦ www.dierksparkside.com

O N A BUSY ROADSIDE JUST SOUTH OF THE HIGHWAY 12 JUNCTION IN SANTA ROSA, IT'S EASY TO MISS THE PARKside Café. But missing it would be a mistake. Owner and chef Mark Dierkhising built his national reputation running luxury establishments in the wine country, and he now serves up the same excellent food in a casual café setting. Passionate about creating unpretentious and imaginative food, with an emphasis on local and seasonal ingredients, the daily breakfast and lunch services at the Parkside are local favorites.

If you want a rare wine-country treat, try to get a spot at one of the monthly Purveyor's Dinners. These evenings — featuring a four-course *prix fixe* menu priced at around $50 a person and showcasing the best foods of the North Bay — are so popular with the locals that you are likely to find yourself the only out-of-towners in the room. With only thirteen tables and one dinner seating, it's an intimate and unique dining experience. It's also a perfect occasion for anyone on a back lane wine-tasting adventure: although there is a small wine and beer list, you are warmly encouraged to bring you own favorite discoveries for service tableside, and there's no corkage fee.

ROSSO'S PIZZERIA
AND WINE BAR

53 Montgomery Drive ✦ Santa Rosa

At *the* Creekside Center

Serving lunch *and* dinner daily *from* 11:30AM *to* 10PM

Tel: 707.544.3221 ✦ www.rossopizzeria.com

ALL THAT FANCY WINE-COUNTRY CUISINE IS WONDERFUL, BUT DEEP DOWN WE ALL KNOW NOTHING ACTUALLY GOES with a fine bottle of zinfandel as well as rustic Italian cooking. That's especially true when the pizza and antipasti happen to come from one of Sonoma County's favorite local restaurants—Rosso's Pizzeria, tucked into a shopping mall where few tourists ever wander. The restaurant is down-home, with daily specials listed on the chalkboard up front and soccer playing on the television in the afternoons, but the co-owners—Kevin Cronin and John Franchetti—come to the business with *haute cuisine* experience, having met over at Napa's Tra Vigne restaurant.

At the traditional lunch and dinner hours, you'll almost certainly have to wait for a seat, but one of the best things about Rosso's is the non-stop service throughout the day. If you are looking for a late lunch, this is the place to go. And in the evening, it's unquestionably worth the wait. The handmade pizzas ($10 to $15) are made in the thin-crust Neapolitan style, with gourmet local toppings, and baked in a wood-fired oven, and there is a tantalizing selection of antipasti, salads, and nightly main course specials (including, in season, oven-roasted Dungeness crab that the locals have embraced with great enthusiasm). The wine list is excellent, with many selections by the glass and very reasonably priced bottles, and there's an emphasis on small wineries that practice sustainable viticulture, both here in California and further afield. If you want to try out one of your recent tasting discoveries, the corkage is just $10 — and the fee is donated to the Santa Rosa United Soccer Scholarship Fund.

CHLOÉ'S CAFÉ

3883 Airway Drive, Suite 145 ✦ Santa Rosa
At *the* Landmark Executive Center
Serving Monday *to* Thursday 8AM *to* 5PM,
Friday 8AM *to* 7PM
Tel: 707.528.3095 ✦ www.chloesco.com

THE REGULARS AT CHLOÉ'S CAFÉ ARE DEFINITELY LOCALS. THIS LITTLE BISTRO IS SET IN THE MIDST OF A BUSINESS park over on the west side of Santa Rosa, and there's nothing precious about the ambiance. In fact, you probably wouldn't know you were in the wine country. The place feels a lot more like one of those small workingman's restaurants you find on the back roads of France, and it's no wonder: The café is owned and operated by the Pisan family, who came to Sonoma County from the south of France back in the 1960s, with generations of experience in the patisserie business behind them. Today, brothers Marc and Alain, along with Alain's wife Renée, continue to make traditional French country favorites using old family recipes.

Each week, there is one featured entrée, a regional French dish that could be anything from a Basque-style chicken (made using locally raised, organic poultry) to *steak frites*. There might be less choice than at some other places, but nowhere in the wine country will you beat the prices, and the food is excellent. The special (great for lunch or an early dinner on Fridays) runs from just $12 to $16. A bowl of homemade soup will set you back less than $5, and the desserts are priced at just $3.

It's the same kind of bargain earlier in the day. You can pick up delicious breakfast sandwiches (croissant soufflé, anyone?) for $3.25, and the lunch menu offers a large selection of sandwiches and salads in the $6 to $10 range, with ingredients running the gamut from duck *confit* to local cheeses. Each week in the wine shop, there is also a featured special that you can pick up at a discount, and Marc is about as knowledgeable a connoisseur as you'll find anywhere. This is just good French country cooking served up with all the passion and none of the fanfare.

WINE SPECTRUM SHOP
AND BAR

123 Fourth Street ✦ Santa Rosa

One block west *of* Highway 101, *in the* Railroad

Square Historic District

Tuesday *to* Thursday 12PM *to* 9PM, Friday *to* Saturday

12PM *to* 11PM, Sunday 3PM *to* 9PM; closed Monday

Tel. 707.636.1064 ✦ www.winespectrum.com

INE SPECTRUM IS *THE* PLACE FOR AFTER-HOURS WINE TASTING, AND IT'S THE PERFECT SPOT FOR A PRE-DINNER drink or some post-dinner entertainment. If a light tapas menu will satisfy, you can make a meal of it here as well. The lunch and dinner offerings ($10-15) range from local cheese and antipasti plates to a smoked duck salad or their delicious chorizo and apple panini. There are also several very good full-service restaurants within walking distance.

When it comes to the wines, the emphasis at Spectrum is on rare and small-lot wines (both local and international), and the tasting menu is extensive. One half of the business, after all, is a high-end wine broker-age. There are usually about forty wines available for tasting, either by the glass or in smaller two- or four-ounce flights — one way to sample the wines from some of the area's small producers if you didn't quite get around to making an appointment. The afternoon when I most re-cently drank my way through a bottle of the local Iron Horse sparkling Wedding Cuvée (less than $40 in the bar), there were also little-known Sonoma and Napa County gems crafted by Tandem, Macphail, V-Twin,

T-Vine, Branham, JC Cellars, Sandler, Lewis Ethan, Valdez, Audelssa, and Radio-Coteau on the list, and the mark-up fee is surprisingly low. If there isn't something available by the glass to suit your fancy, there are also nearly five hundred different wines for sale in the shop. Visitors are always welcome to purchase one and enjoy it in the bar for the bargain price of a $6 additional corkage fee. Most Sundays feature afternoon jazz and live music until close, and on Tuesday evenings local winemakers come in to run the tasting and talk vintages. Blind tasting challenges take place all day on Thursday. The website has complete details. Either way, in the heart of Santa Rosa's historic Railroad Square district, there are antique shops to poke around in, and it's an easy place for a summer evening stroll.

UNDERWOOD BAR AND BISTRO

9113 Graton Road ✦ Graton

Highway 116 *to* Graton Road

Breakfast *and* lunch Tuesday *to* Saturday,

dinner Tuesday *to* Sunday, *and* late-night menu Friday

and Saturday after 10PM

Tel: 707.823.7023 ✦ www.underwoodgraton.com

FOOD & WINE MAGAZINE RANKED UNDERWOOD NUMBER 4 ON THE 2006 LIST OF AMERICA'S 50 MOST AMAZING WINE Experiences, but the gourmet gurus are just discovering what the locals and the areas winemakers have known for years. In those local newspaper polls, Underwood routinely makes a sweep of the Best Restaurant, Best Cocktails, Best Bartender, and Best Wine List categories.

Graton is a small and hopelessly quaint little village on the way out to the Sonoma Coast and an ideal detour if you've been wine tasting all afternoon in the Russian River Valley. The atmosphere at Underwood is country French, with the old nickel-topped bar and big mirrors where you can catch someone across the room in one of those mysterious sidelong glances. The food is French-inspired as well, with everything from oysters on the half shell and a bottle of bubbly (local or imported), to farm-raised lamb and local cheeses. In the summer, there is a small outdoor patio for *al fresco* dining, and the wine list has enough little treasures on it that you might just decide to forgo the driving and arrange your own tasting flight tableside. Dinner entrées are in the $20 to $30 range.

APPLEWOOD INN AND RESTAURANT

13555 Highway 116 ✦ Guerneville

From *the* north, follow River Road west *and* head south
on Highway 116; From *the* south, exit Highway 101 *at*
Highway 12 west, follow Highway 116 north.

Dinner Tuesday *&* Saturday 6PM onward

Tel: 707.869.9093 ✦ www.dineatapplewood.com

I F YOU'RE IN THE MOOD FOR A ROMANTIC DINNER OUT AMID THE REDWOODS, YOU WON'T FIND MUCH MORE CHARMING THAN the restaurant at the Applewood Inn. For more than a decade their wine list (where small back lane wineries of Sonoma County have place of pride) has been recognized with *Wine Spectator*'s Award of Excellence. If you never quite made it as far as the tasting room, here is your chance to try wines made by small producers such as Hanzell, Hawley, Lancaster, Lynmar, Martinelli, Michel-Schlumberger, Nalle, Papapietro-Perry, Pasterick, Preston, Robert Young, Selby, Siduri, Unti, Wattle Creek, and Williamson.

The cuisine blends the best of California with classic French cooking, and if you want a chance to try the celebrated local *foie gras* before it's outlawed in 2012, this is the place to come. It's perfectly seared and served with blood oranges. The menu also highlights seafood and beautifully done meats, making it perhaps not the ideal spot for any determined vegetarians. There are seasonal five-course *prix fixe* tasting menus ($90 per person with wine, $60 without), and corkage is $15 a bottle if you want to open something special you discovered along the way. Entrées *à la carte* are in the $20 to $30 range.

And if you want to pick up the most delicious picnic basket in the wine country, you can order them in advance (48-hours notice, $55 per person). They will include a hamper with everything you need for a picnic at one of the local wineries or a quiet afternoon out at one of the nearby coastal beaches, from the lunch fixings to the corkscrew.

HANA JAPANESE RESTAURANT

101 Golf Course Drive ✦ Rohnert Park

From Highway 101, exit Golf Course Drive east.

Restaurant is *at the* Doubletree Plaza.

Lunch *and* dinner Tuesday *to* Saturday 11:30AM *to* 2:30PM *and*

5PM *to* 9PM, Friday *and* Saturday dinner 5PM *to* 9:30PM

Tel: 707.586.0270 ✦ www.hanajapanese.com

ACCLAIMED BY THE *SAN FRANCISCO CHRONICLE* AS ONE OF THE BEST RESTAURANTS IN SONOMA COUNTY, HANA'S IS the place to come in the wine country if what you want is first-rate sushi done with a California twist. You can choose from a dazzling array of traditional sushi and sashimi rolls — or you can discover some of owner Ken Tominaga's new combinations like unagi and *foie gras*. There is also a good selection of main course entrées that range from marinated black cod and broiled freshwater eel to ribeye steak and pan-seared chicken. The restaurant is located just minutes from Highway 101 in the college town of Rohnert Park, in a small shopping center not far from the Doubletree hotel. The location isn't rolling vineyards, but the décor inside is entirely classy and inviting. Sushi dinners run from around $20 to $45, and most entrées are in the $15 to $20 range.

CHAPTER 5

SONOMA VALLEY
AND LOS CARNEROS

SONOMA VALLEY

Nestled between the Mayacamas range to the east and Sonoma Mountain to the west, the indigenous peoples of California called this area the Valley of the Moon. Today, wine lovers know it simply by the A.V.A. Sonoma Valley. It was here, at the historic mission of San Francisco Solano de Sonoma in the first decades of the nineteenth century, that Spanish monks planted some of the first grapes in the wine country. In 1857, the Count Agoston Haraszthy founded Buena Vista, the state's oldest winery and today a California Historic Landmark. While today Sonoma Highway (12), which runs along the valley floor from Sonoma to Santa Rosa, is one of the busiest tasting routes in the area and home to some of the most famous commercial estates in the county, don't let the big names fool you. Tucked away in corners of the valley — from storefronts on Sonoma's historic plaza to mountain vineyards far up dusty gravel roads — there are dozens of small family proprietors making wines you'll be glad you discovered.

VJB VINEYARDS AND CELLARS

9077 Sonoma Highway ✦ Kenwood

Sonoma Highway (12), 1 mile west *of* Warm Springs Road

Tasting daily 10AM *to* 5PM; estate vineyard tours by appointment

Tel: 707.833.2300 ✦ www.vjbcellars.com

INEMAKING IN SONOMA COUNTY WAS ONCE DOMINATED BY ITALIANS. THESE FAMILIES PLANTED WHAT ARE STILL some of the oldest vines in the region, and they brought with them many of the traditions that characterize the North Bay crush. Then the wine country was discovered. Today, throughout the county, a French winemaking style dominates. Acres of rolling vineyards are planted with chardonnay, pinot noir, cabernet, and merlot grapes.

But if you want to try something different—and something really quite wonderful—VJB Vineyards and Cellars would top the list. The father and son team of Vittorio and Henry Belamonte produces less than four thousand cases of wine a year, sold only through their tasting room, which does double-duty as the local café, where residents stop by to hear

the news or to wait while their car is at the mechanic's. These are wines that the experts agree are special: In just three years—including the 2003 to 2006 vintages—they were awarded more than a dozen gold or silver medals in international wine competitions.

For the curious wine lover, VJB Vineyards and Cellars is a particular kind of adventure. These are wines made from varietals that are hard to find in the United States. In 2005, the family made fifty cases of a delicious aglianico, grown just out behind the tasting room. As far as they know, no one else in the United States grows the grape, and you start to wonder why. Never had a tocai friulano or a barbera? Then you have no idea what you are missing. The focus here is on old-style Italian wines in the best tradition, some crafted from vineyards more than sixty years old and most in the $30 range.

If you come early in the morning, when things are still quiet and the espresso machine is hissing busily, you might get invited to a barrel tasting, a chance to taste winemaking in progress. Or better yet, call ahead for an estate vineyard tour ($20), which includes a personal tasting experience at the Belamonte family home. If you are dreaming of gathering around a table with rolling views of the vineyards — and really, who isn't? — here's your chance.

KAZ WINERY

233 Adobe Canyon Road ✦ Kenwood

Sonoma Highway (12), north *of* Warm Springs Road

Tasting Friday *to* Monday 11AM *to* 5PM

Tel: 877.833.2536 ✦ www.kazwinery.com

KAZ JUST MIGHT BE THE HIPPEST, HAPPIEST LITTLE WINERY IN SONOMA COUNTY. IF WHAT YOU'RE IN THE MOOD FOR is good wine made by a friendly family with an exuberant sense of fun, this is just the place. It's the perfect antidote when everyone around you seems to be taking wine tasting just a little bit too seriously.

The family winery has its origins back in the 1990s. At the time, co-founder Rick "Kaz" Kasmier was a professional photographer with a serious winemaking hobby. He started out making basement wines, and

in 1994 he and his wife Sandi decided to make a go of it. They haven't looked back. At first they poured wines out of the house, then out of some of the local co-ops along Highway 12, and, finally, from the tasting room, which opened in 2003. Today, the business also includes their son Ryan, daughter-in-law Emily, daughter Kristen, and son-in-law Nate.

There's nothing glitzy or pretentious here. Just low-key country charm and a long, shaded terrace where you can always catch a breeze. The vineyards make up the front and back lawns. These are the original vines planted when it was still just a basement enterprise, and the family now sources fruit as well from four of their neighbors (with some grapes from Lake County thrown into the mix). They make mostly reds — Italian field varietals like sangiovese, plus some Rhône-style blends using grenache, malbec, and petit verdot, all in small lots. The total production is just fifteen hundred cases a year, and they don't

distribute. The house red starts at under $20, with most wines in the $30 to $50 range. They also produce three different types of port—a white chardonnay, a blush nebbiolo, and a red blend of barbera, zinfandel, and cabernet sauvignon—all around $30 a bottle and produced under a second label, the Bodega Bay Portworks.

Come anytime, they will tell you, but if you plan your trip at harvest, Kaz is the kind of place where visitors can get a chance to participate in the winemaking process. Try your hand at punching down some grapes on a quiet afternoon. Why not? And if you couldn't quite manage to get away without the rest of the family, kids and dogs are both welcome (juice cartons, toys, and doggie treats are kept in good stock behind the counter). Bring a picnic, pick up a bottle from the tasting room, and relax. It's all good.

MUSCARDINI CELLARS

8910 Highway 12 ✦ Kenwood
Sonoma Highway (12), just north of Warm Springs Road
Tasting daily 11AM to 6PM
Tel: 707.933.9305 ✦ www.muscardinicellars.com

WINEMAKER AND PROPRIETOR MICHAEL MUSCARDINI'S FAMILY HAS BEEN IN THE BAY AREA—AND IN THE WINE business—for more than a century. His grandfather Emilio sold wine in San Francisco after Prohibition and founded the St. Helena Napa Valley Wine Company. Today, Michael is continuing the family tradition, making just fifteen hundred cases a year of mostly classic Italian reds in the $30 to $40

range. He is one of the winemakers leading the way in the revival of sangiovese and barbera wines in Sonoma, and his Tuscan-style "Tesoro" (a sangiovese, syrah, and cabernet sauvignon blend, priced at around $50) captured both a gold medal and the Best in Class award at the Los Angeles International Wine Competition in 2007. The estate wines come from a small one-acre vineyard up in the hills

above Sonoma's Valley of the Moon, but his deep community ties and warm relationships with other local winemakers mean that Michael is also able to source additional fruit from some of the best growers in the county. Conveniently located on Highway 12, right in the heart of Sonoma Valley's most famous wine tasting trail, Muscardini is an easy place to pull over and discover something handcrafted and special. Here, meeting the winemaker doesn't just take place on special occasions: he's usually one of the guys behind the counter pouring your wine. Muscardini shares a tasting room with neighbor and award-winning artisanal winemaker Ty Caton.

TY CATON VINEYARDS

8910 Highway 12 ✦ Kenwood
Sonoma Highway (12), just north *of* Warm Springs Road
Tasting daily 11 AM *to* 6 PM
Tel. 707.833.0526 ✦ www.tycaton.com

TY CATON GREW UP IN SONOMA COUNTY AND MADE HIS WAY BACK TO THE AREA IN 1997, KNOWING EXACTLY WHAT he wanted to do: make wine from the grapes raised on the Caton family ranch and vineyards. Today, less than a decade after his first vintage was released, Caton farms forty acres of vineyards in the village of Agua Caliente, just ten miles south of the tasting room that he shares with his friend and neighbor Michael Muscardini. The total production at Ty Caton Vineyards is just three thousand cases a year, but these small-lot wines have already earned a big reputation. His estate "Tytanium" (around $50), a cabernet sauvignon blend with generous proportions of syrah, petite sirah, and merlot fruit, won both the double gold and a Best of Class award in the prestigious *San Francisco Chronicle* Wine Competition in 2008. The cabernet sauvignon and syrah releases ($20 to $30) have also taken gold and double-gold medals in recent years. But if you can get your hands on it, my favorite is the port-style dessert wine (around $30), which seems to beg for an old leather armchair and a roaring fire.

LOXTON CELLARS

11466 Dunbar Road ✦ Glen Ellen
Sonoma Highway (12) *at the* intersection *of*
Dunbar Road, 2 miles east *of* Warm Springs Road
Tasting daily 11AM *to* 5PM; winemaker tours by appointment
Tel: 707.935.7221 ✦ www.loxtonwines.com

I N THE DRY SUMMER MONTHS BEFORE THE HARVEST, EVEN THE LOW VALLEYS OF SONOMA TURN GOLDEN, AND THE CARS ROLLING down the back roads spin up clouds of dust. Heading up the small lane to the warehouse tasting room at Loxton Cellars, visitors take it slowly. Amidst all the hustle and bustle of an increasingly commercialized wine country, this is a place where the pace is different.

This is the kind of place where proprietor Chris Loxton, a fourth-generation winemaker with Australian roots, will take you out for a walk in the vineyards and give you an education that they would charge you a couple of hundred bucks for over in Napa. Wondering why the rosé is

so unexpectedly dry? Come out the front doorstep, Loxton will say, let me show you those vines. Here, it is all about working with what you have and respecting the inherent qualities of the fruit and the land.

Working is the operative word at Loxton Cellars. This is not a glitzy showroom but a warehouse, winery, and sales office rolled into

one (so if you want the winemaker's personal tour, be sure to call ahead so they can make time for you). The walls are lined with casks, and the tasting room used to be a garage, where the previous tenant built Formula One racecars. You are as likely as not to arrive on a day when something is going on, which is more than half the fun. The staff might be bottling the wines. Or a local restaurant owner might stop by to pick up a couple of cases. With a total production of less than three thousand cases, local restaurants are the only distribution.

The focus at Loxton is on excellent handcrafted zinfandel and syrah wines, in the $20 to $30 range, but be sure to try their port, which is exquisite. It was recently voted the best in Sonoma County.

LITTLE VINEYARDS
FAMILY WINERY

15188 Sonoma Highway ✦ Glen Ellen

Sonoma Highway (12), just north *of the* Madrone Road intersection

Tasting Thursday *to* Monday 11:30AM *to* 4:30PM,

other days by appointment

Tel. 707.996.2750 ✦ www.littlevineyards.com

WHEN YOU WALK IN THE DOOR AT LITTLE VINEYARDS, YOU CAN TELL IMMEDIATELY THAT THIS IS A SPECIAL place, a winery where the music and the laughter are almost as important as the grapes. When you meet Rich Little, you understand why. He's a friendly-looking man with a big smile, and he's happy to take the time to talk. You'll definitely want to hear the story of this family winery and their Band Blend wine, which in 2007 won a gold at the Sonoma County Harvest Fair but sells for a mere $15.

Rich, his wife Joan, and her brother, Ted Coleman—the estate's winemaker—are the proprietors of the Little Vineyards, which started up just a few years back and only makes around two thousand cases of wine a year. But their first four hundred cases won two gold medals and a few silvers in the competitions, and it's been full steam ahead from there. Since there are 100-degree artesian springs on the property, some of that steam is literal. Rich jokes that they don't have to worry about keeping their grapes warm in the winter, and the special microclimate contributes to the hearty estate reds they produce.

The tasting room is also full of local history, and Jack London

enthusiasts especially shouldn't miss out. The heart of the property is a 100-year-old farmhouse that William Randolph Hearst built for his mother, but the bar in the tasting room comes from the old Rustic Inn in Glen Ellen, where those two legendary drinkers Hazen Cowan and London told each other whoppers from 1916-18. You'll also notice the musical instruments over in the corner, and if you come midweek don't be surprised if you find yourself participating in an impromptu jam session. Rich runs a recording studio out of the back of the tasting room, where luminaries like Elvin Bishop have made their music. Rich's band plays charity gigs locally and is a perennial favorite at the Fourth of July party on the Sonoma Plaza that the city hosts every year after the parade.

Little Vineyards focuses on making small-lot red wines, including an award-winning zinfandel, a syrah, and a cabernet sauvignon, most in the $20 to $40 range.

ERIC ROSS WINERY

14300 Arnold Drive ✦ Glen Ellen
Sonoma Highway (12) *to* Arnold Drive, *in* downtown Glen Ellen
Tasting Thursday *to* Monday 11AM *to* 5PM (shorter hours *in the* winter)
Tel: 707.939.8525 ✦ www.ericross.com

THE SUMMERS IN NORTHERN CALIFORNIA ARE HOT AND DRY, AND WINEMAKERS WHO DON'T WATER THEIR VINES WILL find themselves come harvest working with low yields — and with some of the richest and most intense fruits around. It's all part of the trade-off, and here at Eric Ross Winery, where the focus is wines made with minimal interference, some of the un-irrigated fields produce less than a ton of grapes per acre. The results are some terrific Russian River wines ($20 to $35 range), including an award-winning old-vine zinfandel, several pinot noir selections, and — something you won't find every day in the California wine country — a marsanne and roussane blend. The tasting fee is $5, refunded with purchase.

The Eric Ross tasting rooms are located just a stone's throw from Glen Ellen's Jack London State Historical Park, which has a noteworthy museum and some of the best walking trails in the county, with haunting views. The author's daughter used to live in the cottage just out behind the winery, and the tasting room still has a relaxed, home-style feel about it. You can sample up at the zinc-topped bars or over on the big leather sofa, but either way the focus is on a friendly welcome. The winery was started out in the hills east of Occidental by two Bay Area photojournalists, Eric Luse and John Ross Storey, who

used an old hand press for their first vintages. Today the tasting room offers barrel sampling in the spring and meet-the-winemaker events throughout the year.

MAYO FAMILY WINERY

13101 Arnold Drive ✦ Glen Ellen
At *the* intersection *of* Sonoma Highway (12) *and* Arnold Drive
Tasting daily 10:30AM *to* 6:30PM (later than most)
Tel: 707.938.9401, www.mayofamilywinery.com

ITH THREE TASTING ROOMS IN SONOMA COUNTY, IT'S HARD TO MISS THE MAYO FAMILY WINERY, AND WITH all this exposure you might be mistakenly thinking this is a big-time commercial operation. In fact, the Mayo Family Winery really is a family-run business (and that's not

always the case when you see the word "family" in wine country), owned by Henry and Diane Mayo, whose families moved to the county during the Second World War and have made a living, until recently, in real estate. Releasing their first vintage in 1995, they still produce only 10,000 cases of wine a year, and they don't distribute. It's tasting room–only sales.

These are wines still made in the family style. The winemaker, Michael Henri Berthoud, is a Sonoma County native, and his focus is on mostly single vineyard designate wines that run the gamut from a sparkling brut wine made in the *méthode champenoise* ($35) or a gewürztraminer ($30) to classic Sonoma reds (mostly zinfandel). There are more than forty different wines (most in the $30 to $40 range), made from sixteen different varietals, and this means the emphasis is on small lots and handcrafting. Here at the main winery, tasting is at the bar, and it's a good place to start if you're trying to get a feel for the stunning array of grapes used here in the North Bay wine country. If you are ready to move on to reserve-room tasting, try the Mayo Family's second tasting room at 9200 Sonoma Highway (just north of Warm Springs Road on Sonoma Highway [12] in Kenwood; reservations recommended, 707-833-5504). The *Wall Street Journal* recently called their sit-down, seven-course, food-and wine-pairing event "the single best deal in wine country" ($25).

FAMILY WINERIES KENWOOD

9380 Highway 12 ✦ Kenwood
Sonoma Highway (12), one block north *of* Warm Springs Road
Tasting daily 10:30AM *to* 5PM
Tel: 707.433.0100 ✦ www.familywines.com

THE OLD KENWOOD SCHOOLHOUSE WAS BUILT BACK IN THE 1890s, LONG BEFORE SONOMA'S HIGHWAY 12 BECAME one of the busiest wine roads in the county. Today Highway 12 takes you from the town of Sonoma over to Santa Rosa and Highway 101, past some of the most famous names in the wine country. Fortunately, there are still plenty of small producers whose tasting rooms are tucked in among the sprawling estates, and the old Kenwood schoolhouse these days is home to the simply but aptly named Family Wineries, which is shared by more than a half-dozen artisan winemakers. For a $5 tasting fee ($10 for the reserve wines, and either fee refunded with a purchase), you can taste everything from David Noyes tocai friulano to Peter and Betsy Spann's award-winning 2006 chardonnay and viognier blend, which took a gold medal in the *San Francisco Chronicle* Wine Competition. SL Cellars pours a range of fruit-infused sparkling wines (around $25), while Barry and Susan Collier at Collier Falls Vineyards in the Dry Creek Valley produce less than four thousand cases of estate reds, including an excellent primitivo and a reserve zinfandel ($30 to $40 range) that are worth stopping by for.

Also included in the tasting-room collective are wines from the Macrae Family Winery, which makes premium small-lot Russian River pinot noir and chardonnay (around $40). From Tandem Wines come some luscious pinot noir and chardonnay ($35–$50 range) and — something of a rarity in Californian winemaking — a Sonoma Mountain pinot meunier ($60). The grapes were originally destined for sparkling wines made in the Champagne style, but alone it makes a surprisingly subtle red. While you can still visit Christie Vineyards for tasting and winemaker tours up in Healdsburg by appointment (851 Limerick Lane, Tel. 707-431-0662, www.christievineyards.com), you can get an advance preview here.

AUDELSSA ESTATE WINERY

2992 Cavedale Road ✦ Sonoma

Sonoma Highway (12) *to* Cavedale Road, just north

of downtown Agua Caliente

Tasting by appointment

Tel. 707.933.8514 ✦ www.audelssa.com

EVERYONE KNOWS THAT SONOMA COUNTY IS GORGEOUS, AND YOU'LL SEE A LOT OF AMAZING VIEWS AS YOU BUMP along the back roads of the wine country, but if you want to see something that will take your breath away, make the appointment to visit Dan and Gloria Schaeffer, the proprietors at Audelssa. The vineyards and winery are located a long way up a winding canyon road, and Dan will tell you with a laugh that if you think you're lost, just keep going. There's no question that it's worth the drive. When you finally reach the winery, the entire Sonoma Valley rolls out in front of you, and on a clear day you can see all the way to the Golden Gate Bridge.

The wines made at Audelssa are also pretty spectacular. Dan and his father Jean started planting vineyards on these steep hillside terraces back in 1990; today, Dan produces around five thousand cases of estate-grown, small-lot wines, mostly Rhône-style and Bordeaux blends in the $40 to $100 range. For my money, these wines are one of the best back lane discoveries in the wine country and the critics agree. Since 2004, *Wine Spectator*, *Wine Enthusiast*, and *Wine Advocate* have given more than a half-dozen Audelssa wines scores over 90 points. With wine this good, it is no surprise that Audelssa is on its way to cult-wine status, and before long Dan expects the entire case production to be sold by allocation. Already, there are almost five hundred people on the list. If you want to try these wines before there's a wait, now is the moment.

While Audelssa pours wine out of a small tasting room in downtown Glen Ellen (13647 Arnold Drive) from Friday to Sunday, for the full experience make an appointment for a private tasting ($25) with Dan, up on the mountain estate. After, you're welcome to stay and admire the views. With a bottle of wine and the world at your feet, there are worse ways to spend an afternoon.

PETRONI VINEYARDS

990 Cavedale Road ✦ Sonoma

Sonoma Highway (12) *to* Cavedale Road, just north

of downtown Agua Caliente

Tasting by appointment

Tel: 707.935.8311 ✦ www.petronivineyards.com

JUST DOWN THE ROAD FROM AUDELSSA ESTATE VINEYARDS IS ANOTHER BACK LANE WINERY THAT MAKES THE VERY top of my must-see list. You'll know you've hit the home of Petroni Vineyards when you see the Italian flag waving in front of the gates. A visit to Petroni is like a little piece of Tuscany right here in California. Like so many of the Italian winemakers who came to Sonoma County in the last century, Lorenzo Petroni hails from the medieval walled city of Lucca. At the age of nineteen, he started out working in San Francisco as a busboy. Today, the restaurant he went on to build with fellow countryman Bruno Orsi is one of the city's most beloved landmarks: the North Beach Restaurant.

Wine Spectator has long recognized the North Beach Restaurant as having one of "America's Top 100 Wine Lists," and so it shouldn't come as any surprise that before long the Petroni family began dreaming of a country vineyard in the hills of the wine country. In the early 1990s,

Lorenzo knew he had found it: thirty-seven south-facing acres just across a small canyon from the legendary Monte Rosso Vineyards—a hillside estate famous since the 1880s for the superb mountain zinfandel and cabernet sauvignon fruit grown in its red, iron-rich soil. For some, the old stone winery built there in 1886, on what some locals still think of as the old Goldstein Ranch, is where world-class California winemaking began. (Today, Louis M. Martini Vineyards, part of the E. J. Gallo group, owns the property, and if the view from the terrace at Petroni Vineyards isn't enough to satisfy history buffs, visits can be arranged by appointment; www.louismartini.com).

Lorenzo and his wife Maria Elena named the new estate Poggia alla Pietra—the Hill of Rocks—and, in tribute to the family's roots and Tuscany's celebrated brunello, Lorenzo planted the first sangiovese grosso clone in Sonoma. Today, the Brunello di Sonoma ($65) is still the signature wine at Petroni Vineyards, although they also produce a small amount of cabernet sauvignon, syrah, chardonnay, and sauvignon blanc ($25 to $80). They also make an excellent Tuscan-style olive oil ($25) from five varieties of handpicked fruit grown on the property and cold-pressed locally in Glen Ellen. All the farming on the estate is organic, and, with even the machinery running on recycled bio-fuel from the restaurant, Petroni Vineyards is leading the way in sustainable agriculture.

But the hard work of farming isn't what comes to mind when you visit the Petroni Vineyards tasting room. Here, the cypress trees sway gently in the wind and there are stunning views over the Sonoma Valley from the broad terraces. The tasting ($20, refundable with the purchase of six bottles or more) includes some of Lorenzo's absolutely divine homemade prosciutto, fresh bread, and estate-cured olives — plus some of the wine country's most original and delicious vintages.

HANZELL VINEYARDS

18596 Lomita Avenue ✦ Sonoma
Sonoma Highway (12) & Lomita Avenue
Tasting by appointment
Tel. 707.996.3860 ✦ www.hanzell.com

ONSISTENTLY RANKED AS ONE OF SONOMA COUNTY'S MOST PRESTIGIOUS WINERIES, HANZELL VINEYARDS HAS BEEN AT the heart of the wine revolution in California since the 1950s. Making just two wines — a chardonnay and a pinot noir — they have the distinction of maintaining the longest continuous estate production in state history. Hanzell Vineyards last bought grapes in 1962, and today some of their fruit still comes from the oldest pinot noir vines in the New World. This is where quality winemaking in California began after Prohibition, and a visit to this two hundred–acre hillside estate is a unique opportunity to see the past come alive.

Founded more than fifty years ago by the diplomat and industrialist James Zellerbach, Hanzell Vineyards produced its first vintage in 1957, and the intention was always to produce grand cru Burgundy-style wines that could compete with the best wines of Europe. In his pursuit of perfection, Zellerbach was one of the first winemakers in California to embrace some of the new technologies that went on to transform modern enology, including the introduction of French oak and stainless steel tanks. Visitors to the winery today can still tour the historic production facility where some of the first experiments with induced malolactic fermentation began.

Today, the proprietor at Hanzell Vineyards is Alexander de Brye, and the estate produces around six thousand cases a year of what are broadly recognized as some of the most cellar-worthy wines in Sonoma County (typically in the $70 to $90 range). *Wine Enthusiast* rated their 2006 chardonnay 96 points. Occasional special releases are only available to collectors and club members, but private appointments, which start at around $50, include a personalized tasting and a guided tour of a heritage winery that helped to create the California wine country. Reservations recommended a month in advance.

CHARLES CREEK VINEYARD

483 First Street West ✦ Sonoma
On *the* west side *of the* Sonoma Plaza
Tasting daily 11AM *to* 6PM
Tel: 707.935.3848 ✦ www.charlescreek.com

NINETEENTH-CENTURY STOREFRONTS AND CALIFORNIA'S NORTHERNMOST SPANISH MISSION——THE SAN FRANCISCO Solano de Sonoma—— line the historic center of the city of Sonoma and have made "the plaza" one of the wine country's favorite tourist destinations, and if by mid-afternoon you're beginning to see the wisdom of taking your wine tasting pedestrian, a leisurely stroll around the plaza still offers you the chance to make some new discoveries. One must-see place on that itinerary is the Charles Creek Vineyard tasting room, which does double-duty as a local art gallery. Set in an 1890s building on the west side of the square, this is saloon-style tasting, where it's easy to get a bit carried away by the feeling that you are bellying up to a bar in the Old West. Even the wines have Spanish names like Las Patolitas (their 94-point award-winning Carneros chardonnay) or the La Vista cabernet sauvignon, grown on the celebrated Stagecoach vineyards on the eastern slopes of Napa's Vaca Range (also a 95-point winner). The names are a nod to Sonoma's history.

The owners at Charles Creek are Bill and Gerry Brinton, Midwestern transplants with long roots in the farming business. In fact, until the recent public sale, Bill's family was at the helm of the tractor company founded by his great-great-grandfather——John Deere. They planted their first vineyard in Sonoma back in the early 1990s, but only opened the tasting room in 2005, and Charles Creek currently focuses on making chardonnay, merlot, and cabernet sauvignon wines, sourced from Sonoma and Napa counties, including a Sonoma Mountain estate vineyard. They have recently added a small-lot grenache to the lineup. The tasting fee is $5, refunded with purchase, and their wines are in the $20 to $50 range.

CASTLE VINEYARDS
AND WINERY

122 West Spain Street ✦ Sonoma
Just off *the* northwest corner *of the* Sonoma Plaza
Tasting daily 11AM *to* 5PM November *to* March,
until 6PM April *to* October
Tel 707.996.1966 ✦ www.castlevineyards.com

JUST DOWN THE STREET FROM SONOMA'S FAMED THE GIRL AND THE FIG BISTRO, IN A SUNNY LITTLE YELLOW BUNGA-low, you'll find the cozy tasting room of Castle Vineyards and Winery. In 2007, locals voted it the best boutique winery in Sonoma, and, after a long day in the wine country, this is the kind of place where you can plunk down in one of the big armchairs and watch the world go by. There's also a shaded garden patio that is a welcome retreat during the summer, where you can enjoy a tableside tasting experience or relax with a bottle of wine and a picnic.

If you're feeling peckish, you can pair your wine tasting with a selection of local cheeses or with some chocolate truffles —a great complement to Castle Vineyard's range of excellent dessert wines (syrah port and a late harvest viognier, around $35 a bottle). But the main offerings at Castle are their mostly Rhône-style varietals, which range from a dry rosé to grenache, mourvèdre, and syrah wines. Winemaker Vic McWilliams also produces a couple of different pinot noir selections, including a Sonoma Coast and a Carneros. The total case production at Castle is around seven thousand cases, and the wines range from $20 to around $35. It's worth checking their website for special tasting room offers.

LOS CARNEROS

With one foot in Sonoma County and the other foot in Napa, the southern A.V.A. known as Los Carneros — named after the nearby Carneros Creek and meaning simply "the bull" in Spanish — is cooled on hot summer days by the fog that rolls in from San Pablo Bay. The result is a cool-climate *terroir* at the southern tip of the wine country, an area famous for its pinot noir, chardonnay, and sparkling wines. Just minutes from the historic Sonoma Plaza, Sonoma Highway (12)/Highway 121 (the two routes join at the Fremont Road intersection) runs east-west across the appellation and is home to some of the North Bay's most exciting and easily accessible small wineries.

NICHOLSON RANCH WINERY

4200 Napa Road ✦ Sonoma

Sonoma Highway (12)/Highway 121 *at* Napa Road

Tasting daily 10AM *to* 6PM

Tel. 707.938.8822 ✦ www.nicholsonranch.com

RISING UP ABOVE HIGHWAY 12 JUST WHERE THE SONOMA VALLEY APPELLATION MEETS LOS CARNEROS, THE STUCCO visitors' center at Nicholson Ranch Winery gives the impression of a large commercial operation. The estate is undeniably impressive. This is not homespun charm but pure wine country elegance. The tasting rooms are set in the midst of thirty acres of estate vineyards, with spacious windows that look out onto the lake and then beyond to the oak-covered slopes that rise up above the valley. Far in the distance you can just catch sight of the family's private hillside chapel, built in the Greek style by Socrates Nicholson (hiking tours just once a year; ask to be added to the list if you're determined). Today, his daughter Ramona Nicholson, with her husband Deepak Gulrajani, are the owners and proprietors of the family estate.

If the winery is state-of-the-art and luxurious, the winemaking here

is still an intimate and personal affair. The Nicholson family produces less than eight thousand cases a year, and all the wines are made on-site, using a five-level gravity flow system that was specially designed to bring out the delicate complexity of their signature pinot noir wines. In addition to an estate pinot (around $40) and a reserve pinot (around $50), they pour a delicious dry rosé of pinot noir (around $20) that is the perfect drink for a long summer afternoon. Better yet, after your tasting, take a bottle with a picnic out to the lake on the property and settle in to enjoy the views.

At Nicholson Ranch, the emphasis is on wine education and savoring your visit, so there's no need to rush the tasting experience. The $10 tasting fee includes a flight of six wines, and on the weekends, if you managed to miss lunch in the midst of all this eager sampling, you can order small plates of gourmet local cheeses for a modest cost. In addition to the pinot noir wines, Nicholson Ranch is also known for its excellent chardonnay and syrah (most in the $30 to $50 range). After, you can stroll upstairs to the art gallery, which features a rotating display of contemporary California artists, or ask for a tour of the underground caves, which are built forty-five feet into the soil and provide the perfect storage conditions for fine wines in the making.

GRANGE SONOMA TASTING ROOM

23564 Arnold Drive, Cornerstone Place ✦ Sonoma
Sonoma Highway (12)/Highway 121, 10 minutes
south *of the* Sonoma Plaza
Tasting Wednesday *to* Monday 10AM *to* 5PM; closed Tuesday
Tel. 707.933.8980 ✦ www.grangesonoma.com

I F YOU'VE ONLY GOT A WEEKEND IN THE WINE COUNTRY AND STILL WANT TO DISCOVER SOME OF SONOMA'S BEST-KEPT secrets, the Grange Sonoma Tasting Room pours wines for more than a half-dozen premium boutique wineries, all in a beautifully designed space just minutes from the downtown plaza. These are wineries where the production is so small that the estates aren't regularly open to the public, and their proprietors range from industry newcomers in pursuit of their passion to some of the wine world's established talents, looking to craft something special for their own — and your — enjoyment. You won't meet the winemaker over the tasting bar, perhaps, but you might discover your new back lane favorite amid this impressive lineup.

The Grange Sonoma, for example, is currently pouring for Carica Wines, made by Charlie Dollbaum and Dick Keenan, small producers of just two single vineyard designate wines — a sauvignon blanc and a syrah ($20 to $45). The 2006 sauvignon blanc was a gold medal winner at the *San Francisco Chronicle* Wine Competition. Phillip Staehle, the proprietor of Enkidu Wines, specializes in Russian River pinot noir, syrah, and petite sirah vintages ($30 to $40) that have received rave reviews in recent years.

You can also taste the award-winning Sonoma Coast chardonnay and pinot noir wines ($20 to $35) made by Charles Heintz under both the Dutch Bill Creek and Heintz labels, sourced from estate vineyards that have been in the family for more than a hundred years. The total production is under a thousand cases, and, although the vineyards are an exclusively working property, enthusiasts who are willing to make the trek out to Occidental—one of the west county's most picturesque villages—can contact the winery directly for ranch tours (www. dutchbillcreekwinery.com).

Cécile Lemerle-Derbès, the winemaker at Derbès Wines, a native of the Champagne, has a stellar resumé in the wine industry and spent several years as the director of production at Napa's famed Opus One Winery. She is now bringing her experience to the premium wines produced under a small family label—chardonnay and pinot noir wines ($45 range) from Carneros and Russian River vineyards. Eno Wines specializes in a range of small-batch red wines, including grenache and old-vine zinfandels ($30 to $45), and, for anyone who ever wondered exactly how many aromas and flavors pinot noir is capable of expressing, Harrington Wines offers five different wines ($40 to $50) made with the varietal.

At Mantra Wines, the focus is on estate-grown Alexander Valley and Dry Creek cabernet sauvignon, zinfandel, and syrah wines ($25 to $35), made by the Kuimelis family's father-and-son team. It's a familiar story in Sonoma County—the winery started with a barrel of garage wine that ended up being too good to keep in the garage. And the story behind Tallulah Wines was owner and winemaker Ben Davis's dream of making wines instead of selling them. Today the family winery produces single vineyard designate syrah and Rhône-style blends (sourced both in Sonoma County and in Oregon, in the $25 to $35 range) that have earned Tallulah a quick succession of 90-points-plus ratings in the major reviews.

ROBLEDO FAMILY WINERY

21901 Bonness Road ✦ Sonoma
Highway 116 (Arnold Drive) to Bonness Road,
just north of the Highway 121 intersection
Tasting by appointment Monday to Saturday 10AM to 5PM,
Sunday 11AM to 4PM
Tel: 707.939.6903 ✦ www.robledofamilywinery.com

FOUNDED BY REYNALDO AND MARIA ROBLEDO—AND RUN TODAY WITH THE HELP OF THEIR NINE CHILDREN—THE Robledo Family Winery really is just that. From one end of the county to the other, winemakers will tell you that their story is at the heart of what makes Sonoma special. On the back lanes, hard work and talent still count for more than deep pockets and venture capital backing. At the Robledo Winery, that hard work and talent started when sixteen-year-old Reynaldo came to California from his home state of Michaocan to work in the vineyards. Picking grapes paid just over a dollar an hour, and he worked seven days a week to help support his family in Mexico, working his way up to vineyard foreman. After thirty years in the industry, he bought his first thirteen acres of land in Napa's Carneros region in 1984, and today—after just over a decade of running his own winery—the Robledo family makes six thousand cases a year of estate wine, made from grapes grown on three hundred acres of land in Napa, Sonoma, and Lake Counties.

As the first winery in the United States owned by a migrant working family—and as one of the few Latino-owned estates in California's wine country—the Robledo Family Winery is a source of particular local pride in this part of the valley. When the tasting rooms opened in 2003, the mayor of Sonoma declared the occasion Robledo Family Winery Day. Even the president of Mexico, Felipe Calderón, put the tasting room on the itinerary during his visit to Sonoma County.

Those tasting rooms celebrate the family's Mexican heritage. Visitors gather around a long wooden table, and at this family-run business the emphasis is on a warm and intimate wine experience. On quiet days, they are happy to take you out for a vineyard tour, and of course you'll get a chance to taste their wines. Their estate sauvignon blanc (under $20) is a gold medal winner; the Carneros pinot noir took a double gold in 2005. They also source some grapes from Lake County, and that lets the family offer some varietals you might not have had a chance to sample on your back lane adventures — wines ranging from a tempranillo to a pinot blanc and a moscato. The tasting fee is $5, and at 30% their wine club has one of the most generous discounts in the county. The reserve wines (including a collector's edition cabernet sauvignon) go up as high as $125, but most wines are in the $25 to $35 range.

HOMEWOOD WINERY

23120 Burndale Road ✦ Sonoma
Sonoma Highway (12)/Highway 121 east *of the* Schellville Road/
8th Street East intersection, turn south *on* Burndale Road.
Tasting daily 10AM *to* 4PM *and* by appointment
Tel: 707.996.6353 ✦ www.homewoodwinery.com

THE HOUSE PHILOSOPHY AT HOMEWOOD WINERY IS "THE REDDA, THE BEDDA," AND THIS SMALL WINERY IS MORE OR less a one-man show. The heart of the enterprise is Dave Homewood, who started out making garage wines back in the early 1980s, and twenty years later things at Homewood Winery are still low-key and hands-on. The total production is still just around three thousand cases a year, and this is very much a word-of-mouth kind of place, loved by the locals and by weekend visitors from San Francisco. These days, Dave makes about a dozen different wines, ranging from a Russian River sauvignon blanc to a Carneros chardonnay. The reds run the gamut from a Knight's Valley cabernet sauvignon and a Dry Creek zinfandel to a merlot port, all in the $20 to $35 range.

Above all, Homewood eschews all things commercial. The wines are sold only from the tasting room, and it's a point of pride here that there's no advertising budget. Dogs and children are welcome. Tasting is free, and you're welcome to sample whatever strikes your fancy. These are wines that are meant to go with good home cooking, and if you want to pick up a case there's just a simple 20% discount, no need to join a wine club. And those cardboard wine shippers that you might need to get all your discoveries back home? Dave sells them at cost. It's the best deal in the wine country.

THE DI ROSA PRESERVE

5200 Carneros Highway ✦ Napa
Sonoma Highway (12)/Highway 121 (also known as
Carneros Highway), west of Duhig Road
Tuesday to Friday 9:30AM to 3PM
Admission $10 to $15; free Wednesdays
Tel. 707.226.5991 ✦ www.dirosapreserve.org

THE ART AND NATURE PRESERVE ESTABLISHED BY RENE AND VERONICA DI ROSA OPENED TO THE PUBLIC IN 1997, and today it houses an important collection of contemporary art, with an emphasis on Northern California artists. But like so much in the wine country, the estate—which includes more than two hundred acres of wildlife preserve—started out as a vineyard. When the di Rosa family bought the property back in the 1960s, it still included the old winery that once served as the crush pad for hundreds of acres of vines planted before Prohibition. They replanted grapes, renovated the nineteenth-century buildings, and set about growing fruit and collecting art. Eventually, as the collection grew, the vineyards were sold to one of the big commercial outfits in Napa, and the bulk of the estate opened to the public as part of a preservation trust. Today, there are several thousand works of art on display and an active program of gallery tours, special exhibits, and nature hikes to the summit of Milliken Peak, where you can enjoy dazzling views of the Napa River and San Pablo Bay amid the springtime wildflowers and summer grasses.

SONOMA

With its towering palm trees and the historic Spanish mission set off in one corner of the town's central plaza, Sonoma is Old California. In fact, Sonoma is where the Bear Republic that became California began. Walking along the shaded streets and into the town's winding courtyards, it's still easy to feel like you're in another time: a time when the winemakers were ranchers and *padres*, and the road was long and dusty. Today, Sonoma is still the perfect hub for exploring the appellations of the Sonoma Valley, Sonoma Mountain, and Los Carneros.

LASALETTE

452 First Street East, Suite H ✦ Sonoma
Just off *the* east side *of the* Sonoma Plaza
Lunch *and* dinner daily
Tel: 707.938.1927 ✦ www.lasalette-restaurant.com

TUCKED AWAY IN A LITTLE COURTYARD OFF THE EAST SIDE OF THE SONOMA PLAZA, VISITORS IN SEARCH OF SOMETHING just a bit unique in the wine country will find LaSalette, and chef Manuel Azevedo's innovative Portuguese cuisine. Here, you have your choice of patio dining on a warm summer's evening or a cozy table by the wood-fired oven, and the emphasis is on local seafood with a transatlantic twist. The signature dish is a white bean and seafood stew, served in a traditional copper bowl, and they also offer bowls of authentic caldo verde for lighter appetites. The cheese and charcuterie plates are also a tasting treat, and what would any restaurant in Sonoma be without a great wine list? It's a blend of local favorites and some new Portuguese discoveries, including red and white tasting flights and a large selection of after-dinner madeira, port, and muscatel wines, if you're not quite done sampling for the day. Most entrèes are under $25.

THE VASQUEZ HOUSE TEA ROOM

414 First Street East ✦ Sonoma

Just off *the* east side *of the* Sonoma Plaza.

Tea *and* light refreshments Thursday *to* Sunday, 2PM *to* 4:30PM

Tel: 707.938.0510 ✦ www.sonomaleague.org/vasquez.html

ALL ALONG THE SONOMA PLAZA YOU WILL FIND WINDING LITTLE ALLEYS THAT LEAD INTO COOL, SHADED COURTyards, where the early settlers escaped the summer sun in the days before air conditioning. If you wander along the east side of the plaza, you will find the little passageway known simply as El Paseo, at the end of which awaits the Vasquez House Tea Room. Run by the Sonoma League for Historic Preservation, this heritage 1850s cottage is a charming spot, where you can indulge in an afternoon tea, nibble on some homemade pastries, and plan the next stop on your wine tasting itinerary. The house was originally built for the hard drinking and rakish Civil War general "Fighting Joe" Hooker, whose military exploits included the Battles of Bull Run, but whose dashing good looks earned him a reputation for exploits of a rather different character. The library has an excellent collection of early books and artifacts related to Sonoma County history, and the exhibit gallery is worth a peek before you head back out into the sunshine.

THE GENERAL'S DAUGHTER

400 West Spain Street ✦ Sonoma
At *the* corner *of* West Spain Street *and* 4th Street West, three
blocks off *the* northwest corner *of the* Sonoma Plaza
Dinner Tuesday *to* Sunday 5:30PM onward
Tel: 707.938.4004 ✦ www.thegeneralsdaughter.com

IN THE MIDDLE OF THE NINETEENTH CENTURY, SONOMA'S FAMOUS
GENERAL VALLEJO GAVE HIS DAUGHTER 122 ACRES OF RANCH
land as a gift on the occasion of her wedding to Attila Haraszthy—a
man whose father had only a generation before founded California's
first winery, Buena Vista. Today, the sprawling Victorian house that

the young couple built on the land
still stands, and this legacy property
is now home to one of the town's
most innovative restaurants, the
General's Daughter. Out in front,
the palm trees sway gently, and the
long front veranda is about as
inviting as anything you could wish
for. This feels like Old California.

The food, however, is all wine
country. Dinners are served on a
prix fixe basis, with three-, four-,
and five-course menus ranging from
$50 to $75 per person, and recent
offerings have included everything

from Scottish salmon or oysters to venison. During the summer, the General's Daughter offers special winemaker dinners, where you can meet some of the county's most renowned small proprietors in an intimate setting. The wine list is excellent. The emphasis is primarily on introducing diners to the back lane wines of Sonoma, although there is a good selection of wines from around the world. Best of all for anyone who has spent the day out on the wine-country trail trying to select the perfect bottle for dinner, there's no corkage fee for the first bottle of wine if it's not on their list (and $25 otherwise).

CAFÉ LA HAYE

140 East Napa Street ✦ Sonoma
Just off *the* southeast corner *of the* Sonoma plaza
Dinner Tuesday *to* Saturday 5:30PM onward
Tel: 707.935.5994 ✦ www.cafelahaye.com

WITH JUST OVER THIRTY SEATS IN THE DINING ROOM AND A STELLAR REPUTATION, CAFÉ LA HAYE IS THE bustling and intimate kind of place where reservations are a must. In recent years, this local bistro has started getting the sort of big reviews that explain the posh crowd. When you taste the food, you'll understand why the *New York Times* is raving about this little café just off the Sonoma Plaza.

The cooking is California-inspired Italian, with an emphasis on fresh seafood, including a house-smoked trout starter and a daily fish entrée. You can also savor traditional Tuscan pastas, local quail, or a signature hanger steak. The entrées are in the $15 to $25 range, and the wine list features many of the county's most prestigious small producers, along with an extensive (and expensive) list of reserve wines.

WINE SHIPPING SERVICES

ALL WAYS COOL
3350 Coffey Lane, Suite B ✦ Santa Rosa
Tel: 707.545.7450 ✦ www.allwayscool.com

THERE ARE LOTS OF WAYS TO GET YOUR BACK LANE WINE PURCHASES HOME, BUT ONE OF THE SIMPLEST IS CERTAINLY a third-party wine shipping service. Any premium winery can recommend someone to you, and, if you are planning to buy and send home several cases of wine, working with a consolidator can make the whole experience a lot more fun and less expensive. My personal favorite is All Ways Cool in Santa Rosa, which has very smart staff who can also help you down the road when you might want to reorder some of your back lane favorites.

The way it works at All Ways Cool is that you go out tasting and choose the wines you want. Then, you can either collect the bottles in your hotel room, or you can leave your case purchases right at the winery for pick-up later. At the end of your trip, you just need to tell Susan where you've left the wines and where you need them sent. Someone on her staff can come and get them for you from pretty much anywhere in Sonoma County, including at your hotel or B&B. Because you can send all the wines from your tasting trip in one single shipment, it is generally more cost effective than having individual cases mailed from the wineries, and Susan can often arrange delivery to states that don't allow direct shipments from the tasting room.

During the hot summer months, shipping wines to certain parts of the country is a dicey business, and for a small monthly charge per case they will also keep your cases in climate-controlled storage until the cool weather comes. If you are buying futures that need to get fetched from the wineries and mailed in the autumn (and some wineries want you to pick up futures on a particular weekend), this can be an elegant solution. Shipping rates depend on actual weight and location, and as a general rule Susan will tell you that it is much less expensive to ship to a business address. The costs are based on standard commercial shipping rates, plus a modest handling fee. If you are going to do some serious wine tasting and stock up those cellars, this is the way to go.

If you can't get to the wine country or are looking for advice on some good picks to fill out a pallet shipment, Susan also hand-picks a few of her favorite small-production wines each year for distribution to out-of-town clients. So if you need to fill up a case box and never did quite find that perfect zinfandel, you can also count on some local expertise to round out your collection.

WINE COUNTRY SHIPPING

7686 Bell Road ✦ Windsor

Tel: 707.836.7748 ✦ www.winecountryshipping.com

THE FOLKS AT WINE COUNTRY SHIPPING DO MOST OF THEIR WORK FILLING SHIPPING ORDERS FOR SMALL WINEMAKERS, but they also offer delivery services to individual wine enthusiasts and to anyone who might have gone just a little bit crazy with those purchases. Like most of the other shipping services in the wine country, everything about the experience highlights your convenience. Wines can be picked up from your hotel room or dropped off at their offices, as you prefer, and, unlike at most of the shipping companies, the cost of the packaging is included in the fee.

NAPA VALLEY WINE STORAGE

1135 Golden Gate Drive ✦ Napa

Tel. 707.265.9990 ✦ www.napavalleywinestorage.com

MANY OF THE WINE COUNTRY'S MOST SERIOUS COLLECTORS RELY ON NAPA VALLEY WINE STORAGE, WHICH offers high-end temperature- and humidity-controlled storage facilities. But, of course, they also offer a range of shipping services. They will do pick-ups from local wineries in both Napa and Sonoma counties, or you can arrange to drop off cases before heading out of town. And, if you're ending your tasting adventures south of Sonoma along the Highway 12/121 wine route, Napa is an easy — and very pleasant — detour.

INDEX

ABOUT THE AUTHOR

TILAR J. MAZZEO IS THE AUTHOR OF *The Widow Clicquot: The Story of a Champagne Empire and the Woman Who Ruled It* (HarperCollins, 2008) and of numerous other books, essays, and reviews. President of the International Society for Travel Writing and a member of the International Food, Wine, and Travel Writers Association, she divides her time between Sonoma County, California, and Maine, where she is an assistant professor of English at Colby College.

ABOUT THE PHOTOGRAPHER

RAISED ON HIS FAMILY'S VINEYARD overlooking the Dry Creek Valley, Paul Hawley is a wine country native. He graduated from the University of California Santa Cruz in 2003 with a degree in film production. You can find him most days in the cellar at Hawley Winery or behind his lens somewhere along the beautiful back roads of Sonoma County and beyond. Photography and filmmaking remain a passion, and Paul's feature film, *Corked*, premiered at film festivals in 2008.